Binford W. Gilbert, PhD

The Pastoral
Care of Depression
A Guidebook

"**I** found it difficult to lay this book aside! The author holds your interest chapter after chapter. Hopefully, this new resource will better equip us to understand and help persons with depression.

While written primarily for pastors counseling depressed persons, I believe this book also will be useful to busy physicians and to persons who themselves may be depressed or who have loved ones who are depressed.

There has long been a need for a book that clearly states the ways clergy can attend to the emotional needs of persons who are depressed. Dr. Gilbert has written such a book with authority and compassion. I wish it had been available when I began my parish ministry.

In brief, this guidebook by Dr. Gilbert shows depression to be a serious but treatable illness and calls upon pastors to obtain adequate training in order to 'counsel wisely.' Chapter 10, 'Taking Charge of Your Life,' is worth the cost of the book."

Paul R. Beach, DMin
Retired United Methodist Minister,
Belleville, IL

"Dr. Gilbert poses a challenge to pastors to recognize that parishioners may suffer from depression and that depression is identifiable and treatable. He describes how the pastor can identify symptoms of depression, such as sleep interference, anxiety, and psychomotor retardation. He encourages the pastor to action, saying, 'The worse thing you can do for depression is to do nothing.'

Gilbert has been there—he has paid his dues as a pastor, a pastoral psychologist, and a man who personally knows depression. This book is appropriately called a guidebook. Depression is not well understood by many pastors, teachers, and even physicians, for that matter. Yet it is a prevalent problem crossing genders, age, socioeconomic levels, and race. It is identifiable and treatable. When you buy this book, you will want to highlight many passages. Then you will reach for it often.

A less direct message in Dr. Gilbert's wonderful book is that when the pastor personally engages life through helping parishioners, the pastor will be presented a gift, that of seeing himself/herself. Within this integral process the pastor will mature and grow with the parishioner. Ultimately we are one with God, and not 'sick' or 'healthy,' but connected in the struggle to grow. Not a bad deal to receive two for one. Every therapist knows of this benefit."

Ronald L. Riffel, MSW
Social Worker and Business Consultant, Engelwood, CO

"Dr. Gilbert's book is an absolute must for pastors who have served in the parish for a dozen or more years and who are in need of refocusing both their ministry and their personal lives.

As a retired minister who has served the church for twenty-five years, I have learned that you can't export what you don't have. The care and feeding of those personal inner resources is so essential to a continuing effective ministry. This book certainly addresses these concerns. The chapter on 'The Minister's Own Mental Health' opened new vistas for me.

This book obviously has been written by a man who not only has 'talked the talk' but who has 'walked the walk' as well."

J. Bryant Young, MDiv
Retired United Methodist Minister, Houston, TX

"**T**his book will introduce pastors and ministers to the 'common cold' of mental health—depression. It contains practical guides for identifying and dealing with depression as part of a team of helpers, among whom the pastor has a specific role. There are very specific strategies for cognitive and behavioral treatment, all within the context of the pastor's faith and training in theology. There are also very helpful suggestions for the pastor's own personal mental health, with important cautions to avoid common pitfalls. This is a common-sense, down-to-earth book that avoids jargon and clearly defines technical terms in an area that too many seminaries neglect."

Jean Dalby Clift, PhD
Pastoral Counselor,
Denver, CO;
Diplomate, AAPC

"**T**his book addresses with great wisdom and extraordinary experience the treatment of depressive disorders. It is sensitively written, yet pragmatic enough to be of tremendous benefit to anyone presented with the challenge of helping another face the debilitating effects of depression. This book is a valuable resource for any pastor, psychologist, or counselor.

The author presents several instructive approaches to therapy, allowing the treatment provider the opportunity to offer skilled, effective help to those caught in the downward spiral of depression. This book offers a wealth of information about an illness that has reached epidemic proportions. Easy to read, easy to recommend."

Diane D. McKinna, MA
Licensed Practical Counselor
in private practice,
Canon City, CO

"**T**his book provides an accurate description of the disease process of depression, and the way pastors, as caregivers, can respond in a helpful way to those in pain who seek them out. A must reading for pastors from all religious backgrounds."

Barbara Hartman, RN, MEd
Psychiatric Nurse/Mental
Health Counselor,
Northwest Texas Hospital,
Amarillo, TX

The Pastoral Care of Depression
A Guidebook

THE HAWORTH PASTORAL PRESS
Religion and Mental Health

Harold G. Koenig, MD
Senior Editor

New, Recent, and Forthcoming Titles:

The Pastoral Care of Depression
A Guidebook

Binford Winston Gilbert, PhD

The Haworth Pastoral Press
An Imprint of The Haworth Press, Inc.
New York • London

Published by

The Haworth Pastoral Press, an imprint of The Haworth Press, Inc., 10 Alice Street, Binghamton, NY 13904-1580

Cover design by Marylouise E. Doyle.

Library of Congress Cataloging-in-Publication Data

Gilbert, Binford W.
   The pastoral care of depression : a guidebook / Binford W. Gilbert.
      p.   cm.
   Includes bibliographical references and index.
   ISBN 0-7890-0264-7 (alk. paper).
   1. Depressed persons–Pastoral counseling of.   2. Depression, Mental–Religious aspects–Christianity. I. Title.
BV4461.G55   1997
259′.425–dc21
                                                                          97-19563
                                                                          CIP

CONTENTS

ABOUT THE AUTHOR

Binford W. Gilbert, PhD, is an ordained Elder of the Rocky Mountain Conference of the United Methodist Church and a Fellow of the American Association of Pastoral Counselors. Since his semi-retirement in 1991, he has maintained a private practice and was a consultant to a remedial boys' ranch in Colorado. Formerly, Dr. Gilbert was on the faculty and staff at the University of Denver and the Iliff School of Theology. He also served as Director of the Pampa Family Services Center of the Texas Panhandle Mental Health Authority. His ministry career has taken him to several areas of Texas and Colorado.

Introduction

This book is about people, not primarily about an illness labeled depression. The focus is on a process or state called depression, the people who become depressed, and the skilled pastor who chooses to treat them.

What is depression and what are its many and varied types? Who becomes depressed and how can it be recognized? How can it be measured and what are its suicidal potentialities? What are some of the therapeutic interventions a pastor can use in helping people who are undergoing the pain of depression?

Another concern centers around the mental health and strength of the helping professional. The maintenance of a positive, healthy, and even exuberant love for life and people requires self-maintenance. The professional needs to take time to nurture and nourish his or her own soul in order to be able to help others. This becomes a personal as well as professional duty and, in the highest sense, a religious obligation.

Depression is a statistically significant illness in the United States. The age of anxiety has been replaced by the age of depression. It has reached epidemic proportions and appears to be contagious. As early as 1972 a columnist wrote, "Never have so many people been unhappy. A public poll has shown that one out of two people is depressed much or some of the time."[1]

The American Institute of Family Relations points out that depression and suicide have become massive health and social problems among teenagers and young adults. Among youth ages fifteen to twenty-four, more than 4,000 kill themselves each year. Suicide is the third largest cause of death, following accidents and homicides. More alarming is the fact that the suicide rate among youth aged fifteen to nineteen more than tripled between 1954 and 1972.[2]

While accurate statistics are always difficult to come by, the evidence points to a major increase in depression and in the loss of

1

creativity, vitality, happiness, and even life, which follows in depression's wake.

In public mental health facilities, depression constitutes 25 percent of all admissions. In private psychiatric practice and outpatient settings, the figures may range as high as 50 percent (Merck 1992).[3] Of all patients seen in general medical practice, roughly 10 percent are suffering from some form of depressive illness.

Margolis (1995)[4] notes that 8 to 10 percent of all Americans will experience a serious mood disorder during their lifetime. At any given moment, over four million Americans suffer from a major depressive illness.

The costs of treatment, loss of work, poor productivity, permanent disability, and resultant self-medication through substance abuse have an estimated cost between 16 and 45 billion dollars annually.

The economic impact is of great concern, but is overshadowed by the human pain and suffering involved. About 15 percent of severely depressed persons commit suicide (Merck 1992). In the United States, approximately 50 to 70 percent of suicides are due to depression. White males who live alone and who have prior suicide attempts are at the greatest risk. The refusal of treatment coupled with drug or alcohol abuse heightens the risk.

The U.S. Department of Health and Human Services (1993) estimates that "up to 70 percent of psychiatric hospitalizations are associated with mood disorders." One study reported that during a six-month period, there were 4.8 million cases of major depressive disorders. More than 16,000 deaths annually are attributed to suicide.[5]

Stoudemire, Frank, and Hedemark (1986) reported that mood disorders accounted for more than 565,000 hospital admissions, 7.4 million hospital days, and 13 million physician visits annually.[6]

Depression is a treatable illness. What makes the current situation even more tragic is that in many cases, the depression has been identified and is treatable. Depression is one of the most remedial of all emotional disorders. There are many new and effective methods for intervening in a crisis situation or with individuals in a more chronic state of depression.

These methods vary from new drug therapy to counseling and lifestyle change. The hopelessness and helplessness of many depressed persons can be counteracted through modern therapies and techniques now available.

While depression is noted throughout history, it is now highly recognizable and treatable by competent and skilled professionals, including the clergy.

THE PASTOR

Many pastors do not recognize their skills and capabilities in the treatment of mental and emotional disorders and illnesses. Every pastor who deals individually with his parishioners in more than a superficial manner soon learns that many of them are struggling with personal issues that claim much of their energy and sap their lives of joy and meaning.

Sensitive and skilled pastors soon become aware of the lifestyle of self-defeat, loneliness, and pain. Some pastors turn away from talking about deeper issues of life because of their own fear of grief, depression, failure, and despair. The superficial image of positive thinking and external happiness seems to be a mask that many individuals wear. This applies not just to parishioners but also to physicians, psychologists, social workers, lawyers, and pastors.

The minister is often the frontline mental health worker in the community. Various studies have shown that many more individuals seek the counsel and guidance of their minister for personal problems than seek the counsel or guidance of their medical doctor or family physician. Pastors need confidence, competence, and skill in handling people with emotional problems.

Providing a listening ear and a warm, tender heart is a good start, but it is not enough to intelligently solve human problems. One man said years ago that a pat on the back does not cure a broken heart. After someone unburdens his/her life to us, we bear the responsibility of making decisions about further procedure. These decisions will be centered around a working evaluation or diagnosis that will determine whether we will continue to treat the person in pain or refer him or her to another professional. If we decide to work with the hurting person, we must then determine what skills we shall employ and for how long.

If the decision centers around referral, either because of our own time pressures or lack of competencies in specific areas, we must determine the type of treatment that appears most appropriate for the individual.

The Bible is full of references to individuals crying out for help from that reality in the universe which we call God. To read the Bible seriously is to discover that in many situations, people appeal to God for guidance, healing, strength, courage, and wisdom in handling their individual dilemmas and painful situations. Psalm 130 begins with these words: "In my despair I call to you, Lord. Hear my cry, Lord, listen to my call for help!" Only a callous or incompetent (unknowing) pastor would answer that plea insensitively or indifferently.

The pastor is a skilled professional who hopefully brings to bear a caring heart, a keen mind, sharply honed skills, and profound theological and institutional resources that no other professional possesses.

The pastor is a generalist in the broad sense of the term who needs to learn to relate to and work with other helping professionals. The pastor needs to understand the training and background of physicians, psychologists, and social workers and to understand the differences in their personalities and educational backgrounds.

Pastors need to gain a balanced view of the medical profession and realize that in their own arenas, they are or should be as skilled and competent as the medical doctors may be in theirs.

Conversely, many pastors need to lose their messianic complex and realize that they do not have all of the skills and tools needed to help people who are hurting. Naive and superficial clergy often resent other professionals and refuse, because of their own insecurity or ignorance, to open their minds and hearts to other skills they drastically need.

The pastor must be open to teamwork with other skilled professionals. This latter stance can only enhance and increase his/her effectiveness as a human being and as a pastor in the helping and healing of people who touch his/her life.

Therefore, I see the pastor as a helping professional who begins with a set of values contained within, but not limited by, an institution called the church; and as a professional be able to move in and through theological language and to relate knowledgeably to psychological skills. I also see the pastor as an individual profoundly in touch with his/her own streams of consciousness and unconsciousness. In being able to face realistically the pathos and joy of his/her own life, a pastor is able to share in the human enterprise genuinely and warmly.

THE "WHY" OF THE BOOK

Behind the writing of every book there are varied and sometimes hidden reasons and meanings. All books are indirectly or directly autobiographical. Honesty impels conscientious authors to look internally at the reasons for putting their thoughts down on paper and thinking that those thoughts are worthy to be read by other people. This is the case with this book. As a pastor, a pastoral psychologist, and a human being, I have at times struggled with depression, as have most people; my struggles are not unique. Every person who experiences depression needs to know that this struggle is shared with some fifty million Americans. Every human being is different, but we should realize also that we are part of the human race and share in maladies common to the human situation.

So, I must confess that part of the book is autobiographical and originates out of a personal concern to know all I can about this syndrome that affects so many people. The more we know about it, the more we are able to manage, control, direct, and understand this illness. In doing so, we take away some of its power and feel less helpless in the grips of psychological pain. Part of depression may either be caused or worsened by what we do or do not do. Let us therefore seek to take away some of the misery and mystery of this destructive syndrome by shining the light of human knowledge upon it.

I wrote this book to communicate four basic facts:

1. *Depression is a major illness.* It touches millions of lives, robs millions of joy and happiness, costs billions of dollars to treat, affects industry by reduced production, and contributes to marital discord and family strife. These factors alone justify more study and sound research.

2. *Depression is a treatable illness.* Of all the emotional and mental problems (note the distinction between the two), depression may respond most readily to current techniques not previously available. Pastors-central figures in society-need to know about treatment modalities available and how to help individuals overcome their fear of facing the reality that they are depressed, to say the dreaded word, and then do something about their condition, without guilt or self-recrimination about being "ill." Depression worsens when we remain paralyzed to do anything about it.

3. *Pastors are frontline mental health practitioners.* More Americans turn first to their pastors than to their physicians for help with emotional or situational problems. A far smaller percentage would consider going to a mental health practitioner such as a psychologist, psychiatrist, or counselor. The pastor is a significant professional who has access to people in need.

4. *The pastor is unique.* By virtue of skills and training, the pastor occupies an unusual position in society. A pastor has access to people and a mandate to reach out that no other professional enjoys. Most important, the pastor may deal with spiritual, religious, and emotional issues of life and death in unique ways. Issues of the meaning of life and the "why" of things, which often preoccupy the thoughts of depressed people, are within the pastor's sphere of expertise and professional concern.

A farm wife sought help for her husband who had an obvious personality change, felt he was in communication with his deceased family, could no longer function at work, and was in evident pain and suffering. As it was, the man was hospitalized as gently as possible. He was treated for his depression with counseling, understanding, and medication. He recovered and returned to his home and work. His pastor facilitated this process greatly, as well as added a meaningful spiritual dimension and a sense of wholeness. The illness became not only a biological illness, but also an opportunity for growth and insight. Pastoral involvement is essential in treating the spiritual element of depression.

There are basically three types of counseling: insight-oriented, reeducational, and supportive. In severe mental disorder, the pastor must serve primarily in the supportive role, assisting and enhancing the work of other professionals who are the primary caregivers. Coordination becomes essential along with mutual respect and understanding.

When the pastor is the primary caregiver, this book is intended to encourage the following:

A. Action-Oriented Counseling

The worst thing to do for depression is to do nothing. To deny or avoid the illness or its pain is to make it worse. Because of the pastor's unique role, he or she may assist in assertive, action-oriented change and facilitate behavioral modification at appropriate stages of recovery.

B. A Cooperative Relationship with Family, Community, Medical, and/or Psychiatric Community

Treatment of persons suffering from depression is a joint effort. The pastor must surrender any grandiosity or illusion about having a magic wand to solve all of the problems of mankind. Simultaneously, the pastors must surrender feelings of inadequacy and be responsible for adequate training to perform the tasks that are uniquely theirs. This may require consultation, supervision, and guidance. Unless the pastor assumes his rightful responsibilities, his ministry will become or remain shallow and superficial.

C. Responsible and Innovative Creative Therapeutic Interventions

The literature is replete with newer techniques and ideas. The pastor should bring the best intelligence available to solve the problems in his parish. Less than that is unacceptable in a needy world.

D. Treatment of the Whole Human Being

An older physician told a class of young medics that it was more necessary to know what person has an illness than it was to know what illness the person has. Years ago, when I took my first internship in clinical training at a cluster of hospitals, I was reminded of the depersonalization of being ill and being treated like a number (rather than a living, breathing, sentient human being).

The clinical supervisor referred to the "gall bladder on the ninth floor" to illustrate the ease with which professionals slip into this depersonalization when dealing with large numbers of people. It is easy to slip into the habit of referring to people as labels or diagnostic categories rather than as individual persons by name. She is not "that old lady from Cleveland," but Mrs. Jane Doe. People are never labels or diagnostic categories. We may become performers and poseurs in the pulpit, not wanting to bother dealing with humanity one person at a time.

For years, the suffering in former Yugoslavia has been staggering. Every human being should be touched with awareness and pain. A major denomination suggested that those who wished to do so could contribute by sending funds to Cause #478195-K. The fact that this dehumanization came so easily in the name of efficiency makes it even more deplorable. Starving human beings are neither "causes" nor are they project numbers. They are mothers, fathers, daughters, sons, friends, and neighbors. They have names and personalities, purposes and dreams. They are more than numbers.

The clergy, of all professions, is comprised of members who are value seekers and conservators. Let us therefore remember that a human being is the crowning glory of God's creation and should be treated with respect and reverence. Was it not St. Irenaeus who said "The glory of God is a human being fully alive"? We share in the divine creation when we share with God in the healing process. Let the healing begin with us and in us.

Chapter 1

Depression: How It Feels

A distinguished community leader walked into his local church one Sunday morning. He spoke pleasantly with two men and put his hat on the shelf. Instead of turning to his left and going down the hall to the men's breakfast meeting, he walked calmly and quietly into the sanctuary where he stayed alone for two or three minutes. He then left and walked away from the church down the side street, where he took a small gun from his pocket. He pulled the trigger and his life was over.

Was he depressed? If so, who knew about it? What were the outward signs, and could they have been interpreted by family, close friends, pastor, or physician?

A younger man, angry because his wife left that morning due to his drinking and debts, killed himself after having consumed a large amount of alcohol.

A twenty-three-year-old girl, responding to an unfortunate love affair, overdosed on barbiturates after leaving a note for help from her personal hell.

There is a common misconception that suicides are mainly caused by depression. While depressed people may and do commit suicide, there are other clinical diagnoses more accurate for these unfortunate victims. Many depressed people do not take their own lives. Only about 15 percent of depressed persons commit suicide; 85 percent do not. Besides depression, anxiety, neuroses, schizophrenias, business problems, manipulation of others, extreme anger, hormonal changes, or chemical imbalances can all lead to suicide.

Many depressed people lack the emotional and intellectual strength and energy to carry out plans to take their own lives. It is when strength and energy begin to return that suicide becomes a

9

severe threat. Therefore, suicide is more likely to occur in the early stages of depression or in later stages when personal energy becomes more mobilized. Other illnesses and problems, in addition to depression, contribute to the suicide rate.

Depressed persons are usually physically sluggish. They may walk slowly as if weighted down (depressed) with a great burden on their shoulders. Their speech is labored and slow, as though they are searching for words. Mental processes become sluggish and intellectual acuity is, or may be, greatly reduced. Even simple problems, which they may have previously handled with alacrity, become tedious. Adding a column of figures can become a painful chore.

These symptoms, which fall under the diagnosis of psychomotor retardation, are some of the first and most visible outward signs of incipient classical and clinical depression. The mind and body are slowed down to the point that family and friends begin to notice a difference in behavior. For the depressed person, concentration is difficult, if not impossible.

The depressed person begins to lose interest in events that were previously pleasant or appealing. Life loses its joy, and there is little or no desire to respond to invitations or participate in social events. People can suffer from anhedonia (lack of pleasure) without being depressed, but most depressed people exhibit the loss of involvement and responsiveness. This particular stage of depression creates a cyclical response. The more the individual withdraws from society, the more depressed he or she becomes. The more depressed they become, the more uninvolved and withdrawn they are. If this cycle can be interrupted and reversed, we can then move in the direction of healing. This will be discussed in more detail in Chapter 6.

As the depressed person participates less in life's activities and even routine requirements, his or her bodily functions slow down. Less food is desired or required. Food loses its taste and there is little appetite. However, the loss of appetite seems to be disproportionate to the lowered activity rate. The depressed person begins to lose weight, sometimes slowly but surely, and for no apparent reason. Friends may comment that the depressed person looks thinner than usual, or that he or she must be dieting, when actually the person is not even aware of, nor interested in, the continuing weight loss. Weight loss is unintentional and usually of little concern to the individual.

Most depressed persons develop sleep disorders. They previously may have been sound sleepers, but now experience difficulties in getting a good night's sleep. This compounds the onslaught of an encroaching depression by adding tiredness and fatigue to the other problems.

Sleep disorders (insomnia) of the depressed are usually one of three major kinds. The first is difficulty in falling asleep. This initial insomnia occurs repeatedly when the person goes to bed tired but is unable to doze off for several hours. Many times he or she may remain awake and restless all night, sleeping only rarely and fitfully, if at all. The second form of sleep disorder is called intermittent insomnia. The person falls asleep, but awakens one or more times during the night, and may remain awake from thirty minutes to two or three hours each time. The third form is terminal insomnia. This is manifest through early morning waking and the inability to return to sleep, remaining awake until it is time to get up and prepare for work or school.

In many depressions, anxiety is a component and may be involved in the waking episodes. The individual may rehearse frightening scenes or replay and imagine woeful consequences that are envisioned for the future. Doom may seem imminent. Small setbacks and reversals may be magnified to overwhelming proportions. Severe anxiety components in depression are often overlooked by therapists and pastors.

The reverse of insomnia (which is also known as hyposomnia) is *hyper*somnia, the tendency to sleep more than usual. Instead of sleeping too little, the individual may escape from his or her problems and pain by sleeping too much.

One talented young wife came for help complaining that she was sleeping all the time. After a few hours of work in the morning, she would find excuses and ways to take one or two naps in the afternoon and perhaps again in the evening. Then she slept soundly through the night. Once she was able to discuss her internal conflicts and face her ambivalence, she spontaneously discarded her extensive sleep pattern as an unnecessary escape. Her hypersomnia was no longer needed.

Any professional who is sensitive to signs presented by his or her client or parishioner will be aware of sleep patterns as an indicator of disturbance. Hyposomnia and hypersomnia are both to be noted, although hyposomnia or insomnia is statistically more prevalent in depressive disorders. The type or pattern of sleep disorder may be a clue to accurate diagnosis of the form of depression involved.

Perhaps the most outstanding and obvious symptom of depressive behavior is dysphoria. When depressed, a person usually feels so bad that he or she hurts all over. The person will complain of feeling down, sad, alone, alienated, hopeless, and grieving. The depressed individual hurts so much emotionally that the pain carries over into the physical sphere. Depressed people's physical activity is not only slowed down, but their bodies also ache with an unidentifiable and nonspecific malady.

All of us have experienced days in which we did not feel exuberant or happy. These days may flavor our lives and make the good moments seem that much better. The depressed person, however, in her dysphoric state, often does not remember ever having felt well in the past. All she can remember is having been depressed, and she expects to remain depressed in the future. She does not recover spontaneously after twenty-four or forty-eight hours of rest.

Often parishioners or patients will develop a compound depression; that is, they become depressed about their depression and tend to make it worse by ruminating about their painful emotional state.

One woman came to her pastor in such a down mood that she said, "Life is not worth living. I am of no value to anyone else and no one else cares about me or whether I live or die. It is all so hopeless that if I could, I would like to die right here on this spot."

There are certain forms of depression in which the dysphoria is extensively masked. Masked depression has many forms and shapes. Usually, however, dysphoria of the kind indicated above is the overwhelming outward sign of classical depression.

Four other factors are often involved in depression: decreased competency and concentration, lowering of sexual interest, diminution of feelings of self-worth, and vague or sometimes blatant psychosomatic complaints.

A usually skilled and competent professional began to forget his appointments. He would go into his office and tell his secretary that he didn't want to be disturbed. He would sit for several hours trying to concentrate on the work in which he had previously excelled. Slowly but inextricably, he moved into a failure cycle until family and colleagues were able to get him professional help. His loss of competence was an outward sign of an inward depression. He could not concentrate, nor could he produce in ways that had previously been part of his lifestyle.

If all roads lead to Rome, it must also be true that most, if not all, psychic roads lead to feelings of self-worth. Depressed persons may consider themselves too fat or too skinny, stupid, slow, repulsive, unlovable, or unlikable. At some points, their egos have not been strong enough to endure narcissistic injuries or trauma. The rejections of life send them spiralling downward into the depths of self-rejection. The feelings of loss of self-worth are usually very severe and pronounced. The therapist must be able to walk with her patient and outwardly maintain her valuing of the depressed person while he is unable to value himself.

A movie critic at a newspaper reviewed Arthur Miller's play, *Last Yankee*. In her review, she stated that "women's woes seem relatively minor in the scheme of real problems . . . . You want to shake them out of their self-indulgent depressions. . . ."

A reader responded:

> There is nothing "self-indulgent" about depression. It is an extremely painful and debilitating condition, seldom understood by the unafflicted. While I was never institutionalized, my depression was severe enough to prevent my pursuing my career for several months while I was under the care of a psychiatrist. As a lifelong liberal, I have always been concerned and involved with the "real problems" she cites, even during my illness.[1]

Those suffering from clinical depression remain aware of their surroundings and react to them in their usual way, knowing what is expected of them. Nevertheless, possessions, a good job, caring family members and friends, or a social conscience, although desirable and appreciated, cannot pierce the encircling blanket of gloom that is the crux of depression and is nearly always impossible for outsiders to comprehend.

Women seem to be more sensitive to the loss of personal relationships than men. The death of a husband or a family member, or the rupture of a close and sincere friendship will cause many women to become depressed.

Men seem to identify very strongly with their occupations or vocations. Therefore, the loss of a job in which they had invested a great deal of their sense of self-worth can be extremely damaging to the male ego and lead to depression.

A decrease in sexual activity is a sign that the clinician may discover either from the depressed person or his or her spouse. Previous sexual patterns are broken and sexual energy (libido) decreases. In some cases, the person loses all interest or desire for sexual relationships, when they had previously been very active and functioned normally in this area.

The last symptom, but certainly not the least important, is the presence of psychosomatic illness. The term "psychophysiological" would be more accurate since the organ (e.g., colon) is not functioning properly, although the tissue itself is not at this point damaged. However, after many years of being nonfunctional or malfunctional, an organ system may actually become tissue damaged.

For example, an irritation of the stomach, which results in indigestion, can become chronic and result in the development of tissue destruction in the form of ulcers. These ulcers become a protest of the system against the psychological conflicts and disturbances that are going on.

Psychosomatic or psychophysiological disturbances take so many different forms that they are the nucleus of extensive research and study. They can range all the way from high blood pressure, gastric ulcers, ulcerative colitis, migraine headaches, and allergies, to a less specific form of ailment such as chronic fatigue.

Physiological complaints should neither be taken lightly nor overlooked by the pastor or general physician. They should be checked thoroughly to eliminate any root causes or actual bodily illness.

For this reason, the pastor needs to develop close working relationships with physicians whom he trusts and whom he feels are not only medically competent, but humanly sensitive. Pastors must exert every effort to develop and nurture interprofessional relationships for the sake of their parishioners. Many pastors, and indeed many physicians, psychiatrists, and psychologists, are at first uncomfortable in collegial relationships. Pastors at times feel they are in an over-under relationship until they understand the medical profession and some of its needs, fears, and sensitivities. Regardless of this initial discomfort, mutual respect and cooperation is worth seeking, asking for, and cultivating. Ministers should not be surprised (but often are) to learn that medical doctors whom they have placed on a pedestal, have needs and fears just like everyone else.

People who are depressed need the strength and understanding of their pastors in order to move in the direction of healing and wholeness. Clinical depressions hurt and indeed may kill. They need not be as destructive as inaction and incompetence have let them be in the past. Consider the words of one of America's greatest statesmen, Abraham Lincoln:

> I am now the most miserable man living. If what I feel were equally distributed to the whole human family, there would not be one cheerful face on the earth. Whether I shall ever be better, I cannot tell; I awfully forebode I shall not. To remain as I am is impossible; I must die or be better, it appears to me.[2]

Thank God, this continuing suffering is no longer unavoidable. With compassionate and sensitive guidance, there is more hope than ever before that this illness can be managed. Depression can also produce insight and wisdom that can be had in no other way. Nothing is as tragic as a grief (depression) wasted. Let us vow to learn from it, rather than be bound by it. Thank God there is hope-*always hope.*

Chapter 2

The Roots of Depression

The term "clinical depression" is used to describe an entity separate and identifiable from the blues, feeling down, or simple, ordinary feelings of depression. A clinical depression has specific and rather clear diagnostic symptoms that set it aside from other forms of grief or "just being down."

Three factors are always present in psychologically induced clinical depression. First, there is obviously a hereditary predisposition that makes the psyche vulnerable to responses of a dysthymic or dysphoric nature.

Second, there is a history or indication of a childhood background that involves affectional and emotional deprivation. Unreasonably high expectations, along with manipulation by guilt and humiliation, often contribute to the emotional loading that in turn adds to the depression. Encouragement of dependence, inhibition of a healthy expression of anger, and smothering or overly protective parenting may sensitize one toward dysthymia. The latter may be a compensation for the guilt felt by the parent for subconsciously rejecting the child.

Third, there is the presence of an existential situation that provokes stress to a degree that coping becomes difficult, if not impossible, for the already weakened and damaged ego structure. The precipitating event or situation is not necessarily one that would be harmful to another individual with a different genetic inheritance and stronger personality constellation. The depression-prone personality is already vulnerable to life's stresses, which trigger the response of depression or depression-like symptoms.

Leading the list of extremely high stressors are narcissistic injuries of any type. These include events that threaten the individual's self-esteem or feelings of self-worth. Such threats as criticism from valued or significant persons, a decline in salary or loss of a job, rejection in a love relationship, failure to measure up to some standard (realistic or not), or poor performance in an area vested with importance can all produce negative and painful responses in a vulnerable person.

The person who is not prone to depression will take the same events in stride and not react in a negative way. Normal stresses that create anxiety or depression in any human being will cause the nondepressive personality discomfort, temporary dysphoria, and mild depression from which he or she soon recovers in the ordinary course of events.

Being blue, discouraged, or depressed becomes abnormal only when it is prolonged over an unreasonable length of time or the intensity is severe enough to interfere with the person's daily functioning at home, work, or play. Some fortunate individuals seem to be almost depression-proof—often because they have learned through difficult experiences to take the vicissitudes of life in stride. They refuse to be severely depressed or to dwell on the winds of ill fortune.

It is possible to refuse to be severely depressed about most events. We can make decisions about whether or not to be depressed. In some cases, people need to face the fact that they are depressing themselves. In some situations, we choose depression as a response, even though it is an inappropriate and painful one. We therefore can learn to choose another response that is more appropriate and healthier. In a later chapter, helping people learn to be depression-proof will be discussed.

There are a few basic causes of depression. First, an endogenous (originating from within) depression is caused by changes within the individual and is not primarily the result of emotional stressors or psychological causes. This type of depression may often be the most severe form experienced in clinical practice. There are no evident situational factors that bring about the dysphoria or other presenting symptoms.

Competent pastors or clinicians will spend adequate time to gently explore environmental and life factors until they are comfortable that there are no situational stressors capable of producing the current problem. Also, time should be spent investigating the individual's response to his or her depression.

Endogenous depressions are sometimes compounded when the pastor or therapist does not help the person deal with his reactions to what is going on in his life. This understandable emotional overlay causes one to be depressed because one is depressed—a painful and unnecessary side effect that may be prevented. Most depressed people feel helpless to do anything about their depression. Helplessness and hopelessness assert themselves as major symptoms and problems. This compounding of depression results when the person realizes how terrible she feels and begins to think that this is the way she will be the rest of her life.

In endogenous depression, a thorough physical examination and often referral to a competent psychiatrist are mandatory. Do not assume that the psychiatrist is competent in this area because he possesses a medical degree. Check his credentials, reputation, sensitivity, and his willingness to work in a collegial and consultative relationship. Determine the method or methods he uses in the treatment of depression. Check with medical colleagues for their responses to his handling of depressed individuals.

Endogenous depressions may be caused by several occurrences within the person. They may be precipitated by hormonal changes, illness, lack of nutrition, medication, aging, strokes, or even certain neoplasms such as pancreatic cysts or tumors. The inhalation or absorption of toxic sprays in large doses may create an endogenous type of depressive illness.

Whatever the cause, the origin is not primarily psychological or emotional. It is medical and should be clearly treated as such. If the medical profession errs in trying to treat all emotional problems with medication, the ministry often errs in treating biochemical problems with prayer or counseling. Clearly, pastors are least helpful to parishioners in pain when they (the pastors) attempt to provide inappropriate treatment. Treating an endogenous depression with only prayer is incompetent and hurtful. Clearly, the ministry has more tools available than that. An old adage states that if your only tool is a hammer, then you tend to see every problem as a nail. We need to develop more tools and skills in the treatment of people in pain.

This in no way means that the pastor or psychotherapist should relinquish her involvement and/or support. This is an ideal time for holistic and cooperative collaboration in helping a person return to optimal functioning.

Another type of depression, which is related to the endogenous type, is the bipolar (i.e., two poles) or manic-depressive syndrome. As its name implies, the mood or affective state fluctuates from the manic phase of ebullience, optimism, grandiosity, enthusiasm, and often excitement to that of despair, discouragement, dejection, and severe dysphoric clinical depression.

We all have a manic-depressive cycle. In most of us, the mood swing is not marked or overly significant. Some days the world is full of beauty, joy, and excitement. Other days, work becomes dull and monotonous. As the old hymn says, "Life is tedious and tasteless." Routine becomes drudgery and life is not quite as exciting as we might wish it to be. The ordinary and very normal human being experiences fluctuations in mood, which are as much a part of life as breathing.

If we could measure our moods on a scale from 1 to 10 with 1 being the lowest and 10 being the highest, most of us would spend the majority of our days clustered around 5 with a variation now and then of plus or minus one or two points.

For a manic-depressive, or more correctly, for someone suffering from bipolar mood (affective) disorder, the chart would be much more dramatic. The highs would be higher and the valleys would be lower. The manic-depressive cycle would be much more dramatic and erratic than that of a nonbipolar individual.

The length of the cycle varies with the individual as does the variation from the midpoints. For some, the intensity may vary severely from the norm, while with others, the intensity is not as marked. The length of the cycle also varies. One person who is ill with bipolar disorder may spend days elated and then plummet to the depths of despair overnight. Another might spend weeks or months in the up phase before switching to the opposite affective pole.

Manic depression is thought of as a biochemical illness, treatable primarily with a simple salt, lithium carbonate. Due to the toxicity of the chemical, it should be closely and regularly checked for accuracy of dosage. Too little will have no beneficial effect and too much will be injurious. A therapeutic level of lithium must be maintained.

Again, the treatment must be that of medical intervention. This must not be interpreted, however, as the signal for the pastor or therapist to refer and abandon. There are definite psychological and spiritual problems involved that must remain the province of the responsible pastor or counselor.

In some contemporary clinical and psychological research, there is indication of personality patterns that may be involved with the manic-depressive patient. Most of the research, however, is incomplete in this area. For the time being, bipolar illness remains a medical problem that should be treated as such.

A third category to be explored is that of exogenous (originating from outside the person) depression. These would include affective disorders in which the primary causative factors are emotional, cognitive, or situational in nature. In exogenous depression, the root causes are thought to be external to the individual.

Labeling various types of exogenous depression is very confusing and often erroneous. It is much more helpful to realize that depression is not caused by external situations, but rather by the individual interpreting external situations in such a way as to become depressed. The concerned pastor will be aware of some of the behaviors, attitudes, and emotional roots that contribute to mood disorders.

In theology as well as science, we must make the distinction between necessary and sufficient causation. An unfortunate event such as death or failure may be a precipitating factor in the development of a problem. The event itself is very seldom the cause. It is our interpretation of the event that creates the response.

The personality that has had a precarious childhood, full of insecurities and traumas, may function quite well until later in life when an event triggers a major illness. The event itself is the presenting problem, but underlying the situation is a vulnerable personality that has been thrown out of balance. The individual's basic constitution (genetic inheritance) has childhood history superimposed upon it, which becomes intertwined into the adolescent or adult personality. An existential situation or series of situations occur that can strengthen or weaken this personality. If this person is fragile along certain lines and life becomes overwhelming, they will break down with a major depression. The current situation is a result of all three factors: genetic inheritance, childhood history and personality factors, and existential stressors. Any one of the above factors may be necessary to precipitate the illness, but, in and of themselves, they are not sufficient.

A skilled clinician, as well as a competent pastor, will seek to treat all three forces. The pastor may be the last generalist left upon the professional scene. The privilege and responsibility becomes incumbent upon him or her to treat the parishioner as a whole person: body, mind, and spirit. To treat the body and neglect the spirit and will of the individual is inadequate. To treat the spiritual part of the person without concern for the bodily or biochemical factors may also be improper. Let us therefore combine our skills in an effort to assist our parishioners to reach toward their fullness as human beings. We are created by a loving God who seeks through all of life to move us in the direction of health and wholeness. There are resources within us and around us to aid in that spiritual growth.

Chapter 3

The Subconscious and Depression

"Out of the depths have I cried unto thee, O Lord."

Psalm: 130

For many centuries, writers have been aware of the phenomenon that today we commonly call clinical depression. St. John of the Cross wrote of the dark night of the soul. Dante speaks of it in literary terms. John Bunyan was no stranger to it. Explorations into the causes and roots of depression have been made for centuries.

In order to attempt to understand the deep recesses of the human mind and soul, the pastor must be aware of the sacred ground that is being explored. The subterranean labyrinthine caverns of the mind hold clues to some of the driving forces behind depressive episodes. We enter into the sanctity of another human being's life with fear and trembling, or more appropriately, with awe and reverence. We do so only by invitation that is delicately granted when trust has been achieved. Here, the pastoral therapist treads lightly, always preserving the dignity of the person and the sanctity of the relationship.

To view depression from the psychodynamic model is to seek the underlying psychological "causes" of the illness. What developmental stage was arrested? What emotional content thwarted? From whence does the pain or trauma originate? Is there one traumatic event or were there a series of traumatic events? Was the person wounded in ways that remained quiescent until he or she erupted in a full-blown illness? Whatever the questions, the focus is on the inner private life of the parishioner. The search is for "secrets" that, when woven together, may create the riddle of the pain now being confronted.

We are more susceptible to being or becoming wounded at certain stages of our lives than at others. Abandonment at three years of age may be more significant than at seventeen. Divorce or death of a parent may be excruciatingly painful for a child at fifteen, but not as severe at a later age. Stages of development must be always kept in mind, with the understanding that what is important is what the event meant to the individual: how it was perceived by him/her at the time as well as in the present. Keep foremost in your mind the question "What did the event or situation mean to the person when it was experienced?" What does it mean to the person now as his or her life cycle is viewed from a more adult or mature perspective?

Depression is often coupled with or related to grandiosity. Grandiosity as used here indicates that the self has established grandiose or expanded views of the person, often in order to compensate for diminished feelings of self-worth. Indeed, psychoanalyst Alice Miller sees some depression as the reverse of grandiosity. "In fact, grandiosity is the defense against depression, and the depression is the defense against the deep pain over the loss of the self."[1]

Depressives see themselves as failures because they do not, or did not, live up to expectations of themselves or those placed there by an internal mother image that can never be satisfied. The similarities are best spelled out in Miller's own words:

> They have many points in common:
> A false self that has *led* to the loss of the potential "true self"
> A fragility of self-esteem that is based on the possibility of realizing the "false self" because of lack of confidence in one's own feelings and wishes
> Perfectionism, a very high ego ideal
> Denial of the rejected feelings (the missing of a shadow in the reflected image of Narcissus)
> A preponderance of narcissistic cathexes of objects
> An enormous fear of loss of love and therefore a great readiness to conform
> Envy of the healthy
> Strong aggression that is split off and therefore not neutralized
> Oversensitivity
> A readiness to feel shame and guilt
> Restlessness[2]

Thus, depression can be understood as a sign of the loss of the self and consists of a denial of one's own emotional reactions and feelings. This denial begins in the service of an absolutely essential adaptation during childhood, to avoid losing the object's love. For this reason, depression indicates a very early disturbance. Right at the beginning, in infancy, such persons have suffered from a deficiency in certain affective areas that are necessary for stable self-confidence.

The important thing for the pastor to remember here is that the causes of the pain are sought in the inner sanctum of the subconscious or unconscious mind. The cognitive therapist and the behavioral therapist would approach the study from an entirely different point of view.

Miller would see depression as the loss of the true self, the inability of the person to be who and what he or she really is, to feel and express what is really going on within him or her.

Freud, on the other hand, would approach depression as a result of separation or grief. To Freud, depression represents loss of a loved one or thing. However, he distinguishes grief from melancholy (literally: black bile) by stating that in grief, there is not the depreciation of the self, self-disgust, or loathing, as there often is in depressive disorders.

> Mourning is regularly the reaction to the loss of a loved person. In some people, the same influences produce melancholia instead of mourning and we consequently suspect them of pathological dispositions. The distinguishing mental features of melancholia are a profoundly painful dejection, cessation of interest in the outside world, loss of the capacity to love, inhibition to all activity, and a lowering of the self-regarding feelings to a degree that finds utterance in self-reproaches and self-reviling, and culminates in a delusional expectation of punishment. The disturbance of self-regard is absent in mourning; but otherwise, the features are the same.[3]

Many pastors feel compelled to reject Freud largely because of misinterpretations or misunderstandings of his writings. One older student in a psychology class that I was teaching remarked to the class that Freud was "one sick puppy." Certainly, Freud had his neuroses like most of us, but his pioneering insights into the dark, foreboding continent of the human mind should not be hastily rejected. The important things pastors should seek to note and remember about

Freud are his labeling of the structure of the human personality (id, ego, and superego) and turning the light on the unconscious or subconscious mind. Things are not always what they seem on the surface, and pastors, of all professionals, have observed that.

RAGE

In psychodynamic studies of acute depression, the component of *anger* has frequently arisen. If an individual becomes so angry at his or her spouse, or boss, or the world, that the anger cannot be controlled, he or she often turns it inward upon the self. This turned-inward anger (retroflexed anger) is so powerful that even physical paralysis can take place in an effort to control the rage. Rage is not too strong a word to use here since it is exactly what many depressed people feel inside.

At this point, the pastor can be extremely helpful, especially if he is working collegially with another trained professional such as psychologist or psychiatrist. We are taught as Christians to love one another, to be kind and gentle, to learn humility. We are usually taught, either directly or indirectly, that good Christians not only control their anger and negativity but that if they are mature in their Christian faith, they will not even feel anger toward another human being or event.

Much of that stems from a misunderstanding of the scriptures. We are enjoined to "be angry but sin not," and Jesus becomes very angry when the house of prayer, the temple, is being perverted by the money changers. We will later deal in more detail with open and harmless ways of dealing with anger. The pastor must theologically understand that it is healthy, natural, and even very scriptural to feel and express anger. Bottled-up anger is one of the potent explosive devices residing deep within many outwardly kind and gentle parishioners.

"RAGE"

Rage, rage, rage, rage on you anger of life,
rage on about pain, loneliness, injustice, and strife,
rage about poverty, illness, and death,
rage until your fury runs out of breath.

Rage is creativity gone mad
it is energy dissipated into insanity
to cover up all that is sad.
Rage, rage, rage on you anger of life,
it does little good except to keep you from pain,
if you run fast enough powered by rage,
your loneliness will seek you in vain.
Rage, rage, rage, rage on,
until you know it does no good,
it only serves to make you hurt
and destroy the good.
Rage until you drop and drag,
rage until your life force is exhausted
anger is the false mask of impotence,
it is a poor substitute for power.
Rage, rage, rage on you demon of destruction,
you ambassador from hell,
you merciless whirlwind of energy gone wild,
rage on in temper tantrum like a little child.
Rage on, it is but a poor substitute for life,
to cover the pain of rejection, the loneliness
of who you are
weak, powerless, rejected, isolated, and all those
phony, cover-up words of self-pity, of poor me,
of ain't it awful.
Words that conceal your inability to face up to life;
to look it in the face and spit in its eye,
rage on, but always remember, rage hurts only you,
at least internally.
Rage is the source of your own destruction,
rage is the source of destruction of love and tenderness,
rage destroys friendships and loyalties,
rage is the substitute for your own weakness,
and hesitancy to stand up and be independent and responsible.
Rage, rage, rage, rage on,
but you hurt only yourself,
those you love,
those that you would befriend;

remember it destroys joy in life,
energy to create, and touches the memory of laughter
until it becomes hate.
Rage on if you want to destroy
sanity, peace, power, tranquility;
rage on, but it doesn't solve your problems
or cover your weakness
or soothe your pain.
Let go of your rage only if you want to become free,
responsible, guiltless, happy, powerful and competent;
rage on if you want to keep your anger at life,
rage on if you want to stay melancholy and sad,
rage on if you want to destroy and hurt,
rage on if you want to be a pain to those that know you,
rage on if you want to destroy love, friendships and self-respect. (Bin Gilbert, 1994)

DEPENDENCY

During and perhaps even prior to the illness, the depression-prone individual may be more clingy, dependent, and responsive to the need for others than the average person. This dependency can extend far back into childhood where the need for security was never met or satisfied. Constant reassurance became a necessity, as the child had to reach outside of himself for the reassurance that he was loved, acceptable, and secure. When the external props are removed, the internal props (ego strength) are not adequate to nurture and sustain the needy child and, later, the adult.

The approval of others is sought more ardently than the inner approval from oneself. Often, this type of person becomes subservient, and indeed a servant of others, in order to allow him or her to gain a needed role in life. Inner strength, in and of itself, is not deemed sufficient.

The *Diagnostic and Statistical Manual of Mental Disorders* (DSM-IV) classifies individuals who have undue attitudes of dependence on people and things outside themselves as having a Dependent Personality Disorder. The Merck Manual uses the term "dependent personalities." These people permit the needs of others to supersede their own needs. They lack self-confidence and initiative, and are often more than willing to turn the major decisions affecting their lives over to others. During episodes of illness, they feel intense discomfort when alone for more than brief periods. They may surrender major responsibilities for their ongoing day-to-day living to someone else.

This phenomenon is most evident during acute depression, and must be handled with delicacy and firmness. As people become stronger, they must learn to again assert control over their lives. Their lives are their responsibility, and that responsibility should never be assumed by someone else except temporarily and for brief periods of time.

The pastor must walk with the depressed person, but at the same time, realize that he is teaching that person to walk for himself. Assistance is offered until the person is able to take back control of his life. The ultimate goal of all therapy is to help people make decisions for themselves, to stand on their own feet, and to become self-actualized, fully alive human beings.

PESSIMISM

In general, the basic formula for depression is $D = S + P$. The S stands for sadness and the P for pessimism.

> The pessimistic component is the essential part of the formula. It is the patient's conscious or unconscious neurotic idea that what happened to him now will always continue happening, or that the condition in which he has found himself will never change. This pessimistic attitude, this inept attempt by the patient to forecast his future, is one of the factors responsible for turning sadness into depression.[4]

Jules Masserman, former president of The American Psychiatric Association, discusses in his perceptive book, *Theory and Therapy in Dynamic Psychiatry*, man's quest for ultimate assurance in a perfect and benevolent world. In order to find this kind of cosmic security (which does not exist), we construct the fantasies and myths that we need in order to survive. These ultimate fantasies or illusions are developed in the service of obtaining a perfect world where we are not overcome or confronted with overpowering fears.

The first of these fantasies centers around an illusion of physical invulnerability and possible immortality. This helps to counteract the unthinkable terrors of death and annihilation. Masserman points out that all of medicine is a "quest for strength and longevity."[5]

Second, there is the illusion of and quest for *brotherly love*. This idealized dream of peace and tranquility arises in the frightening awareness that the world is and can be a hostile place to live. In order to counter that knowledge, we develop religions and ideals that highlight the hope of brotherly love. Perhaps not until we confront the reality of the hostile environment in a tense political scenario, whirling through space in a vast cosmos, can we then become aware of and respond to the many benevolent companions in life's journey.

Third, Masserman points to our quest for a celestial order. In order to defend ourselves from an imperfect world in which we have imperfect knowledge, we as humans create an *ur* (ultimate) defense and an assumption about perfect wisdom that can discern order, security, and benevolence in a universe of chaos and disorder. This is or often may be accomplished by creating myths about sciences, philosophies, or even religions that promise us this perfect cosmos. If and when these fail us, we can then resort to intercession of omniscient, omnipotent, and omnipresent "beings" who can be controlled or manipulated by metatechnology—"beings," who as Masserman points out, "can be controlled by wheedling, bribery, or command, much as one once controlled one's parents."[5]

Any discussion of depression must pay attention to the feelings of helplessness and hopelessness felt by the parishioner or patient. Seligman describes helplessness as the "psychological state that frequently results when events are uncontrollable."[6]

Depression then results when the subject has, or feels that she has, little control over her situation and the reaction to her environment. In other words, the outcome of her actions or of her life are unpredictable and unrelated to what she does or does not do. Results, for the depressed person, become factors of chance.

SUMMARY

1. Most reactive depression is "caused" by some sort of traumatic event. Be careful about the word "caused." The trauma

may be the trigger or precipitating event, but only one of the factors in the causative complex.

2. Past events provide the psychological foundation or personality constitution to create exaggerated reactions to stress of a depressive nature.
3. Patients have been made hypersensitive and vulnerable to the specific traumatic event by losses and traumas of the past.
4. The stronger the ego, the better the individual can absorb traumas.
5. Insecurities of the past, and unendurable situations of stress to which they were exposed in childhood, make certain individuals vulnerable, or more susceptible, to depressive syndromes and symptoms than others.
6. Various old anxieties may be remobilized by current stressors.
7. A major stress is the fear of losing love (acceptance) and of being deprived of the "narcissistic supplies" necessary for life.

Erik Erikson certainly realized the importance of the epigenetic sequence in the development of the child. He pointed out that a drastic loss of accustomed mother love without proper substitution at this time can lead (under otherwise aggravating conditions) to acute infantile depression or to a mild but chronic state of mourning which may give a depressive undertone to the whole remainder of life. But even under more favorable circumstances, this stage seems to introduce into the psychic life a sense of division and a dim but universal nostalgia for a lost paradise.[7]

An interesting side comment might be that this resembles the lostness and alienation in the story of Adam and Eve being evicted from the Garden of Eden. The loss of innocence, when cherished idealism is surrendered, can be excruciatingly painful. We leave the garden of perfect delight to learn to live in a world of challenge and pain. Realistic hope, solid faith, and shared pain and love become powerful and real, perhaps for the first time in the individual's life. We can, and must, move through depression, to the radiant awareness of peace, power, and hope.

Chapter 4

Making the Diagnosis

THE DIAGNOSIS

Making a diagnosis is an arbitrary assignment of categoric labels of discrimination that enable the pastor or therapist to intelligently research, discuss, and counsel the individual. Diagnostic labels assist in understanding the process that is taking place within the person that presents himself for help. Labels may also be constrictive in that they may encourage tunnel vision, i.e., we see only what we want to see and what is included in the diagnostic category.

Always remember, labels are for canned tomatoes, peas, or carrots, not for human beings. The labels serve a tentative, although helpful function. Human beings are always more than the names we attach to them. A label provides only a temporary aid to "getting at" or "getting within" the person's life framework.

Diagnosis becomes necessary in order to communicate with another professional, family member, or the parishioner. Categorization assists in helpful treatment planning. Solid diagnostic evaluation is the foundation for a successful plan of action. It also enables research and may be helpful in providing background information on the type of malady involved. Naming the pain may also be helpful in giving us and the parishioner a perspective with which to view the depression and what is going on within himself. We can assist the hurting person by objectifying his problem—putting it "out there" as an entity to be explored, understood, managed, and overcome.

Depression is a very treatable illness, and we benefit from knowing as much about it as possible. It is an important point to help the person realize the distinction between "having a depression" and feeling the despair of the depression having them. The pain can become an objectified problem that the person can learn to change and therefore manage.

As stated earlier, many depressed people develop a compound or secondary depression when they realize how bad they really feel. They become depressed about their depression and feel that they have always and will always feel this bad. The caring pastor can counteract this hopeless feeling and bring hope and courage to replace the helplessness.

Properly handled, the initial phase of exploring the history and antecedent events without expressing fear can impart hope. At this first stage of exploration, a calm, secure environment that portrays competency and strength on the part of the pastor is essential. Severely depressed people need someone (e.g., a pastor, family member, or physician) and something (e.g., the church, faith, or medicine) to hold onto until they can find strength within themselves. We must walk with them and sometimes for them until they can walk by themselves. The pastor serves best when he or she lends his or her confident strength to the hurting parishioner.

False reassurance can be harmful and should be used sparingly, if at all. A pat on the shoulder with shallow affirmation may cause further loss of strength and confidence in someone who is acutely depressed.

In making the differential diagnosis of depression, the pastor begins by observing and listening. Observe the walk of the parishioner. If possible, go out to the waiting room and walk with them slowly to your office. Is their gait slow or rapid? Is their stride steady and confident or weak and uncertain? Do they have trouble deciding where to sit in your office? Do they choose a chair close to you or far away? How are they groomed? Are they disheveled, hair unkempt, with clothes sloppy and dirty, or are they fastidiously groomed, neat, and clean?

How are their cognitive processes? Are they thinking clearly and rapidly or are their thought processes confused and foggy? Are there difficulties in remembering names and dates? Are there rapid flights of ideas or rapid speech with disjointed and disconnected thoughts?

The basic task here is to learn to observe. Let the pastor give the parishioner the gift of attendance, complete focus on the immediate meeting between two living beings. Attendance simply means being there. Being there not just in body, ready for an obligatory appointment, but being there in mind and spirit, willing and able to concentrate on the significance of the moment. Put aside the bills due, the quarrel with your spouse, or the tasks scheduled for the week. Learn to attend, to be there for the person you are with. Observe, listen, and seek to understand and enter into the other person's world. Learn to place the burden of yesterday and the anxiety over tomorrow on the shelf and be there for another person as completely as humanly possible.

"Blessed are you who have eyes to see, and see: and who have ears to hear, and can hear" (Matt. 13:16).

The *Diagnostic and Statistical Manual of Mental Disorders IV* (DSM-IV)[1] clearly lists the criteria for affective (mood) disorders. The pastor will more likely be presented with dysthymic or major depressive disorders than some of the other symptoms or syndromes, so let us first look at unipolar affective disorder—depressed mood.

1. Sleep Disturbance

There is a variance from the usual or customary pattern of sleep. These can vary, as mentioned earlier, from sleeping too little or too much, having trouble falling asleep, or early morning or intermittent awakening.

In most cases of incipient depression, there is a sleep pattern disturbance, the type or form of which should be noted for further reference.

2. Weight Change

While most texts will highlight weight loss of a dramatic nature as a primary symptom, family physicians and internists are as likely to point out weight gain as a sign of depression. Dramatic, involuntary weight change, not due to dieting, in either direction, should be noted.

One professional lost forty pounds in a little over a month when suffering from an encroaching major depressive episode.

3. Sexual Desire

A person struggling with inner issues of depression experiences diminution of libido or sexual desire and performance. Interest in the mate and in other persons in general declines. The capacity for intimacy, emotional and physical, wanes, and the symptomatic parishioner could care less about sex. The individual usually shows very little concern over this symptom, and the complaint may come from the spouse or significant other.

As in weight change, sexual libido can escalate as a defense mechanism (reaction formation) against loss of desire or performance. This is more unusual, and less mentioned, until it gets to a noticeable proportion, and may be the beginning or part of a hypomanic episode.

4. Dysphoria

The term simply means "to feel bad," burdened, weighted down, depressed. Some depressed people in rare instances do not experience the primary feeling of dysphoria but deny or repress (mask) this feeling, and it emerges symptomatically in other ways. Usually, however, the first symptom noted by family, friends, and business associates is a sad, discouraged, and often painful expression. As one friend told the other, "You have a defeated look about you." The person walks looking down at the ground, the eyes are sad, even tearful. If asked how he is feeling, he will respond with vague expressions of worthlessness, failure, discouragement, and often despair. Some will deny or make light of this symptom, not wanting to admit how bad they feel, as if they could keep it from the outside world.

Persistent sad or empty moods are primary markers of depression.

5. Psychomotor Retardation or Agitation

The most common outward sign is slowed speech, walk, or movements not customarily attributed to the individual in previous activities. Thought processes are slowed and the parishioner walks as if it is difficult and painful to do so. Muscular activity is notably changed and family or friends encourage him or her to hurry and keep up. It becomes difficult for the depressed person to do so. Often, significant others lose patience with the individual and may interpret the slowness as laziness, lack of effort, or a "put-on."

In more rare instances, the person seeking help is agitated, cannot sit still, talks too rapidly, and appears so restless that it is hard to get and hold his or her attention long enough to decide on appropriate courses of action.

6. Self-Reproach and Inappropriate Guilt

Depressed people become overwhelmed with self-recrimination and indeed incrimination. They feel that their depression is a sign of their weakness and inferiority, that people will see what inferior, unworthy people they are. They often feel that the depression is their fault and that if they were made of sterner and stronger stuff, they would not feel this way. Inappropriate guilt is expressed in many ways. Grandiosity often comes out at this stage, as if the person assumes responsibility for the entire world.

One very conscientious and moral woman began to excessively obsess about having neglected her mother ten years earlier. Her mother had died after a long illness, during which time the daughter had lovingly cared for her. Years later, the daughter could remember only that she could have done more, that her mother felt that she had been neglected. None of these feelings had basis in fact. No reassurance could change the feelings. As the depression lifted, the daughter was able to see more clearly that she had been a good daughter and had done everything humanly possible.

These feelings of unworthiness, inappropriate guilt, and inadequacy can reach delusional proportions. These feelings need to be taken seriously, not glossed over with pious platitudes.

7. Inability to Concentrate

Have you ever had a severe headache and tried to complete your income tax forms? Or been overwhelmed by children needing your immediate attention and tried to carry out business tasks? The depressed person experiences extreme difficulty in performing mental tasks that usually do not constitute a problem. A woman that is depressed cannot keep her mind on her job as a lawyer or a housewife, and her performance declines noticeably. As the depression lifts, and some do spontaneously, performance in cognitive realms improves. The poor performance that is a result of the depression should be viewed with patience and understanding.

8. Fatigability

When a person who is usually active and efficient begins to move in the direction of a clinical depression, he often may complain of being tired most of the time, of having very little energy, or of being fatigued without apparent reason. There are many other problems, both medical and psychological, that can precipitate this symptom. For that reason, the informed pastor must care enough to gather a large enough picture of what is going on before including the fatigability as part of the depression. Again, a good place to start is with a compatible, cooperative physician who can rule out a physiological or medical basis for the fatigue.

9. *Anhedonia*

Hedonism is derided as an evil in some denominational groups. Indeed, to them, the worship of sensual pleasure or immediate gratification is a sign of shallowness and immaturity. On the other hand, life without pleasure is not worth living. The Greek origin of this word (anhedonia) simply means the absence of pleasure; life has lost its flavor and literally nothing seems to have meaning for the depressed person.

Where previously the individual has responded excitedly to any number of events or activities, there is now no interest in anything. Even eating, friendship, or sports lose their enjoyment. This may become so pronounced that it is difficult to get the person with a "vital depression" activated or motivated to participate or respond to anything. The individual acts as if life is not worth the effort.

In the cognitive study of depression, there is a rule of thumb called the cognitive or negative triad. A depressed person has a negative view of self, a negative view of the world, and a negative view of the future. Imagine how flat and hopeless a person must feel when depression has reached this level.[2]

It is not helpful—in fact, it is harmful—to try to argue these feelings away. Cheap or superficial affirmations of positive thinking do more harm than good. The pastor should take seriously what the parishioner is saying. Allow the parishioner's negativity, but do not necessarily agree. The parishioner needs to feel the strength of the pastor and/or physician when his own hope has eroded and is temporarily lost.

Each of the above criteria can be measured along a continuum—from no evidence of the symptom to extreme manifestation of the problem. If five or more of these symptoms are displayed in moderate to severe form, the diagnosis of clinical depression can then be made with confidence. If helping professionals are available, they should be contacted for consultation.

The pastor should be careful about consulting professionals without the specific permission of the person involved. Even when specialists are brought in or consulted, the pastor should maintain the privacy and sanctity of the person's shared secrets. Only the symptoms and relevant data should be passed on, preferably only when there is a written release allowing the pastor to talk to another about the subject's problems.

There are exceptions to confidentiality. Suicidal ideation or attempts need to be communicated to relevant family and/or professional colleagues. Although the pastor can lose some popularity for getting involuntary help for the troubled person, the individual and family will be grateful at a later date. Popularity is not the point; saving someone's life is the point. Confidentiality should always be used in the best interest of the person and must be breached only in times of imminent danger to physical health.

A second caveat about confidentiality is where the life or well-being of another is threatened. A husband in a jealous rage who leaves the pastor's office declaring that he is going to harm his wife, ex-friend, boss, or whomever places the pastor in a dilemma. However painful the decision, if the pastor feels that there is real danger to another, he has the duty to warn the other party involved and, if necessary, to call the police or other relevant authorities.

A third caveat involving confidentiality concerns the neglect or abuse of a child. If there is clear evidence that a child is being molested, sexually or otherwise, or severely neglected, this must be reported to relevant authorities such as a department of social services. The parishioner should be informed that you will, and must, report these incidents.

In the initial visit, if possible, and later during ongoing sessions, the pastor should be up-front about the matter of confidentiality. The sanctity of the parishioner's confidentiality is inviolate with the three exceptions mentioned above. The pastor must at times struggle with hard choices about when and how to take action; but as a competent and conscientious professional, these choices must be made.

Chapter 5

Cognitive Therapy

"STINKIN' THINKIN'"

At times, it seems the more obscure and complicated something is made, the more the general population seems to think it is profound. The bumper sticker that read "eschew obfuscation" was not only good humor, but wise insight. Cognition loosely refers to the way in which we know and understand (cognize). When we use simpler terms, it sounds either cutesy or flippant. It is not intended to be either.

Perhaps it was Zig Ziglar who first used the term "stinkin' thinkin'" in one of his motivational books or lectures. Whomever it was, the idea is sound: The way we think can make us sick, poor, unhappy, lazy, or just the opposite. We can learn to think differently and therefore change our lives.

A study of the Stoics strongly indicates that it is not situations or events that upset us so much as it is our interpretation of them. The way we have learned to respond to or interpret circumstances may shape the way we feel. Our thinking can mold, influence, and even determine the way we feel. Thoughts influence emotions.

Please notice that I used a softer phrase: "thoughts influence emotions," rather than "thoughts determine emotions." We can become so entrenched in specific ways of thinking and reacting that we are unaware that there are options other than the ones we have chosen. In that case, thoughts become unconscious and automatic. As sure as night follows day, the emotional reaction will be consistently the same unless something intervenes to interrupt the cycle.

It is this cycle of unconscious thought equaling automatic response that cognitive therapy seeks to intercept and interrupt. Do not let the term "cognitive therapy" intimidate you. It refers to

41

"stinking thinking": ideas, assumptions, and attitudes that are automatic, consistent, and unconscious until they are brought into the light of day. These myths are irrational thoughts by which we live, move, and have our being.

The early behavioral psychologists developed the formula S = R: stimulus equals response. Change the stimulus and you change the response. Later behaviorists added an additional component to the formula: S + O = R, or stimulus interpreted by the individual organism produces a response. They were recognizing that human beings are more than simple machines, and that they may influence how they respond to certain stimuli.

Let me give an example. A death occurs. The family is distraught, shocked, numb, and in grief. One member of the family is aware of the lengthy suffering that preceded the family member's death and the pain that would have been likely in the future. This mourner loved the deceased no less than the others, but was grateful for the long and productive life that had been lived, the beauty and wisdom that had been shared, and the joy that came into the world because this one person had lived. He or she also knew that this individual who died was ready to go, wanted to die, rather than live as an invalid, in pain for the rest of his or her life. The way the death was interpreted makes significant difference in the way it was responded to. In addition, the beliefs held by the family and friends about an afterlife, God, guilt, and punishment influenced the grief process.

Another family member, no closer to the deceased than the first, interprets death in an entirely different way and with an entirely different set of cognitive beliefs. To this person, the death is interpreted as abandonment-as a cruel blow administered by an arbitrary and hostile God. Her loved one was taken, plucked up, as it were. She approaches the death from the standpoint of her loss, as well as the termination of the life of the other person. Anger results as one of the defense mechanisms, and the individual lashes out at the impotent medical system, heaps guilt on other family members for not caring or doing more, and becomes debilitated while facing the pain of her own mortality. She becomes "alone and afraid in a world she never made." Her cognitive beliefs are entirely different; therefore, her emotional reactions may be entirely different.

One set of beliefs leads to equanimity in the face of death. Another set of cognitions leads to overwhelming pain. The grief-stricken relative may even feel that he or she should be in severe distress. If not, it would mean to the person that he or she did not truly love the deceased.

Let us look in some depth at some of the structure of cognitions and automatic, irrational thoughts that we all live with.

There are too many times in life when we are not in control, when we are not even captains of our own souls, when we are not and cannot be masters of our fate. Twenty years ago, while suffering from a major depression, I became painfully aware that my attitudes and emotions were not always at my discretion. They were influenced by hormones, circumstances, historical events of time and place, physical health, neurotransmitters, and chemicals, over which I had little authority at that time. My dependence at that point was on people-experts-outside of myself to help me regain control of my attitudes, emotions, and health. So, the myth of invulnerability must be one of the first myths to be questioned in the pantheon of personal beliefs.

Let me hasten to say emphatically that this does not give us an excuse to not exercise our own power and responsibility when possible. There is never the prerogative to say, "I can't help myself." We have no right to abrogate the power and responsibility that we do have.

Years ago, while pastor of a small church in Houston, I came across the writings of Albert Ellis. I was struck with the practical wisdom of his psychology. Having been schooled heavily in Rogerian person-centered counseling, I discovered that for some problems, Ellis' rational-emotive therapy was far more practical for use with parishioners. His basic thesis is that irrational ideas may not only cause emotional upsets, but may also prolong and maintain them. He pointed out eleven basic dysfunctional thoughts that could create difficulties for some of us.

- **Irrational Idea 1.** The idea that it is a dire necessity for an adult human being to be loved or approved by virtually every significant other person in his community.

- **Irrational Idea 2.** The idea that one should be thoroughly competent, adequate, and achieving in all possible respects if one is to consider oneself worthwhile.
- **Irrational Idea 3.** The idea that certain people are bad, wicked, or villainous and that they should be severely blamed and punished for their villainy.
- **Irrational Idea 4.** The idea that it is awful and catastrophic when things are not the way one would very much like them to be.
- **Irrational Idea 5.** The idea that human unhappiness is externally caused and that people have little or no ability to control their sorrows and disturbances.
- **Irrational Idea 6.** The idea that if something is or may be dangerous or fearsome, one should be terribly concerned about it and should keep dwelling on the possibility of it occurring.
- **Irrational Idea 7.** The idea that it is easier to avoid than to face certain life difficulties and responsibilities.
- **Irrational Idea 8.** The idea that one should be dependent upon others and therefore needs someone stronger than oneself on whom to rely.
- **Irrational Idea 9.** The idea that one's past history is an all-important determiner of one's present behavior and that because something once strongly affected one's life, it should indefinitely have a similar effect.
- **Irrational Idea 10.** The idea that one should become quite upset over other people's problems and disturbances.
- **Irrational Idea 11.** The idea that there is invariably a right, precise, and perfect solution to human problems, and that it is catastrophic if this perfect solution is not found.[1]

Albert Ellis was a pioneer, a giant in exploring new realms of counseling and psychotherapy. Pastors will quickly realize his focus upon stoic philosophy.

Paul Hauck, also a clinical psychologist, perhaps with more understanding of and appreciation for the church, added a twelfth irrational idea.

• **Irrational Idea 12**. The idea that beliefs held by respected authorities or society must be correct and should not be questioned.[2]

We will be examining more dysfunctional ideas further along, and begin to understand what makes these ideas "irrational" and how they may be recognized in our own lives.

According to rational-emotive therapy, any thinking is rational, and therefore healthy if, when acted upon

a. it assists you to survive.
b. it most likely will result in the preservation of your life and limb rather than your premature death or injury.
c. it produces your personally defined life's goal most quickly.
d. it prevents undesirable personal and/or environmental conflict.[3]

Rational thinking is intended to achieve the goals and values you select to make your survival pleasurable, enjoyable, and worthwhile. It is always important to note that psychotherapy must take into account the individual's value orientation.

If rational thinking is designed to enhance life and achieve goals, we may then theorize that irrational thinking will not do that, but rather be antilife, unhealthy, and opposed to wholeness (holiness), happiness, and growth.

Most emotions serve an ongoing function for the person involved. The skilled pastor will ask himself what "payoff" is involved in staying mad, jealous, envious, or self-righteous. When the economy of the emotion can be determined, then the question can be asked of the parishioner, "Do you feel that it is worth it to continue that response to this situation?" Jealousy is often used as a projection to cover up a person's own lust. Anger, which continues, has no useful function except to cause an illness in the stomach or elevated blood pressure. If the emotion no longer serves a useful purpose, then is the patient/parishioner willing to look at the possibility of giving up the emotion that is no longer appropriate or economically necessary? If they are, then we can rethink the situation and find more suitable and healthy emotions for the one being given up.

Do not deify or focus upon the list of irrational ideas formulated by Albert Ellis or Paul Hauck. Determine for yourself what constitutes a "dysfunctional idea" or irrational assumption. Be willing to examine them in the light of new, adult information, and to create new assumptions when the time is right.

The Jesuits have always produced significant scholars that are worthy of attention. John Powell, SJ, is one such scholar who offers profound Christian insight and help. In *Fully Human, Fully Alive*, he lists seventy-five cognitive distortions that are important to every religious person seeking to live a growing and enriching Christian life. He challenges us to take a new look at our visions of the world, of others, of self, of the future and, in the process, develop a more dynamic framework for ourselves and others. Pastors should examine and reexamine themselves regularly as they help others to grow spiritually.

A major assumption that most people make is that things or people "make us" the way we are. How many times have you heard, "He makes me so mad" or "When it rains, it makes me so depressed?"

No one makes us anything. They do not have that power unless we give it to them. The rainy sky may contribute to our feelings of sadness or inertia or melancholy, but it certainly does not have the power to control our emotions unless we choose to let it. Certainly, some situations are more unpleasant than others, but when we invest others with the power to determine our emotions, we surrender control of our lives to someone else. The center of gravity no longer resides within us, but we voluntarily, perhaps unconsciously, hand it over to someone else.

People coming into the church or the mental health clinic often focus on the power and control others have had over their lives. The basic task of the pastor and/or counselor is to help the patient/parishioner get out of the victim role and take responsibility for his/her own life. Do not surrender control of your own emotions. Your mother or mother-in-law, bishop or church or difficult parishioner does not control your emotions unless you let them. Nobody can "get your goat" unless you give it to them.

One courageous and kindly pastor had polio since adolescence. In spite of that, he completed college, then seminary, married, and fathered children. He spent a productive life making the world a better place. He aided society in making the world safer and better for people with handicaps. When he died, the obituary stated that he was a "victim" of polio. That statement was patently false. He was a victor over polio and decided that he would control his emotional and spiritual destiny rather than surrender to self-pity or passivity. Anyone who wants to look deeply into the scriptural foundations for this position has but to read the works of Paul the Apostle seriously: "Nay, in all these things we are more than conquerors through him that loved us."[4] There is not always an easy answer or quick fix for our problems, but new ways of thinking and acting can pave the way to a rich life with reasonable composure and tranquility.

Thinking processes usually accompany, precede, follow, and sustain or extinguish human feelings. It is upon these automatic, unconscious, nonproductive thoughts, ideas, or myths that cognitive therapy focuses its attention. In rational-emotive thought, we are responsible for creating, continuing, and modifying our thinking and emotions. We change emotions by changing the way we think about events and situations.

The way we use language impacts our emotional life by reaffirming or denying the emotional consequences. We may interpret events, situations, and circumstances as horrible, terrible, awful, or intolerable. As a result, our negative emotions escalate and we become even more upset. If we can learn to change some of our interpretative language we can change some of our emotions. For example, to have a root canal is an unpleasant event not often sought by people. We may describe to ourselves how catastrophic and horrible the pain will be so that we become extremely apprehensive and our anxiety makes the situation worse than it should be. On the other hand, we can accept the fact that the procedure is unpleasant but soon will be over, and that it is well within our range of tolerance. Our anxiety level then drops to manageable levels and we begin to see the dental procedure as therapeutic rather than catastrophic.

Ellis outlines the A-B-C Theory of Emotional Disturbance:

- **A** — Activating Experience
- **B** — Belief About
- **C** — Upsetting Emotional Consequences
- **D** — Disputing Irrational Ideas
- **E** — New Emotional Consequence or Effect

Your girlfriend breaks the news that she is seeing someone else. She wishes to terminate her relationship with you. You interpret the experience as a personal rejection and tell yourself that you are a worthless, undesirable person and that you will never in your life find someone who wants or needs you. This particular girlfriend is the only one in the world that can meet your needs. On the other hand, you could get very angry and tell yourself that she was a conniving, untrue woman with low ethical/moral standards, and that you hope she gets what she deserves. As a result of these interpretations, you generalize and tell yourself that this is a horrible experience, and that it always happens to you. You are either a repulsive person, or the girlfriend deserves to have bad things happen to her.

Also as a result of your interpretations, you become very angry (hostile) or depressed and begin to feel miserable. Most of us have had unpleasant experiences that we have made worse by our interpretations of them. Beliefs about the situation obviously compound any negative emotions we have. In the majority of cases, beliefs about the situation are automatic and unconscious. To learn to interrupt and modify these beliefs then becomes the major task for us.

With either our own efforts or the help of a skilled and concerned counselor, we can learn to examine our assumptions and automatic beliefs. They may be reevaluated on the basis of whether they are helpful or not, whether they are true or not, and whether or not we wish to modify them in any way.

At this point, many people say, "I can't help the way I feel." Or perhaps they tell themselves that they cannot control their emotional reactions. Some practice and effort is needed, but changing one's feelings can and is done every day by many intelligent people.

One very devoted wife in her early forties came into the mental health clinic very distraught because her husband had moved out of the house. The family had been very active in a conservative church and divorce was severely frowned upon. Further, the man of the house was the boss, only slightly lower than God and the angels. They had three daughters who were in high school and each wished to go to college. The faithful and dutiful wife began having panic attacks, became severely depressed, and openly expressed her feelings of helplessness. Somehow, she had failed her husband, she thought. What would "cause" a man in his mid-life situation to move out? She must no longer be desirable as a woman. She worked hard at her job, and in the home, did everything she could to please her husband.

Still, her husband chose to move out of the home. In effect, he said, "I don't want to be married anymore." Instead of facing his responsibilities, he went out and bought a new luxury sports car and moved into an apartment in a single's complex. The man's wife was overwhelmed. The two oldest daughters were rather indifferent to his absence, while the youngest missed her father but was angry at him.

In the midst of the wife's pain were her powerful feelings of dependency. She often said that she couldn't live without him, did not know what was she going to do now that she was alone, etc. On one depressing day, the client was feeling exceptionally helpless and dependent. By this time, the counselor had worked with the wife long enough to know that she was a good employee, well liked at her job, a capable mother, and that she possessed adequate personal skills when she would use them.

Cautiously, the counselor inquired about who dressed the woman for work that morning? Quizzically, she responded: "Well, I did, of course." The question then was asked who got her out of bed that day, and a similar answer was given. Then she was asked who did her work for her at the office. By this time she was becoming irritated at the line of questioning. Finally, she realized what was happening. She had come in with tearful eyes, feeling helpless. Slowly, she became irritated at the counselor for asking such dumb questions, and then she began to laugh. "I see what you are doing," she said. "I guess that I am not as dependent and helpless as I had come to think. I don't need that chauvinistic jerk to complicate my life. I deserve better than that." A turning point had taken place in therapy and from that moment she began to grow toward a more healthy lifestyle.

A caution here: paradoxical intervention or counseling should be used carefully, if at all, and then only by a skilled pastor or counselor after a trust relationship has been established. Prematurely or unwisely used, paradoxical therapy can be harmful to the counseling relationship.

Aaron Beck, a psychiatrist, led in the treatment of emotional disorders through his research and the development of the cognitive model. Some of his basic premises are very similar and are related to the rational-emotive model of Ellis.

In both systems, the emphasis is placed on the way we think about events and the words we use to ourselves and to others to create and maintain these emotions. In his classic book, *Cognitive Therapy and the Emotional Disorders*, Dr. Beck explains the difference between the conditioning model of the early behaviorists, the method or system of the psychoanalytic model, and that of the cognitive approach.

The early behavioral model would look something like this:

Stimulus = Response

The psychodynamic model would introduce an intervening variable and look like this:

Stimulus + Unconscious Thought = Response

The cognitive model would change the intervening variable and look similar to this:

Stimulus (event) + Conscious Thought = Chosen Response

In the behavioral or conditioning model, the stimulus to an emotion comes from outside the self, i.e., it is external. In the psychoanalytic or psychodynamic model, the stimulus is internal but unconscious, i.e., not in conscious awareness. Therefore, the behavior is due to factors about which the person is unaware. In the cognitive model, the emotional responses are related and due to specific meanings we give to events. Arousal is an aftermath of interpretation placed upon the situation, and through common sense observation; therefore, we may sort out and change these specific meanings.

For Beck and others, these new ideas slowly replaced earlier hypotheses. "The new formulations gradually eased out the psychoanalytic theories that I had been taught and believed: that depression is caused by hostility turned against the self and anxiety is stimulated by the threatening break into consciousness of a taboo (forbidden) wish."[5]

Rather than delve deeply into the subconscious, the focus is placed upon conscious, automatic thoughts that are dysfunctional and need to be reexamined in the light of new evidence and current (adult) reasoning. Modern therapy techniques owe much to the wisdom and groundbreaking ideas of people such as Albert Ellis, Maxie Maultsby, Paul Hauck, Aaron Beck, and David Burns. Beck developed the Depression Inventory, which has gained wide usage across this country.[6] I recommend that every pastor order copies of these people's works and keep them on hand to be used in specific situations.

David Burns, in his book *Feeling Good: The New Mood Therapy*, includes a dysfunctional attitude scale. Permission should be sought from the author to duplicate this and any other instruments that may be copyrighted. I have found ethical and compassionate clinicians such as Hauck, Lewinsohn, Beck, Maultsby, and Burns to be extremely helpful and generous in their permission to utilize their material, when appropriate.

DYSFUNCTIONAL ATTITUDE SCALE

An excellent guide for group therapy of depression is Burn's book. Several instruments contained in it are worth becoming familiar with in order to utilize them in group settings. Perhaps the most important is the worksheet on harmful attitudes.

Burns points out seven areas or clusters of emotional needs that are or may become harmful and lead to painful and dysfunctional living. These needs are approval, love, achievement, perfectionism, entitlement, omnipotence, and autonomy. This DAS (Dysfunctional Attitude Scale) allows the parishioners to discover areas within themselves that may not be as productive and life-enhancing as they would like them to be.

The answers can then be interpreted and scored to indicate emotional strengths as well as areas of vulnerability. In that way, the parishioner can discover and examine each cluster to determine if the values they have lived by are ones they wish to change or continue. Some people will choose nonhelpful attitudes and will want to continue to live with them. Others will recognize and review their feelings and decide they no longer function within a productive and therapeutic framework. They decide to work at changing them, thereby alleviating their despondency. Remember, the key concepts:

1. Some depressions are learned responses to stress.
2. What was learned can be unlearned or relearned.
3. Changing your attitudes and thoughts will change your depression.

Pastors should familiarize themselves with the techniques of rational-emotive therapy, cognitive restructuring, paradoxical intervention, and other documented and effective methods of assisting people in changing painful and hurtful patterns in their lives.

The pastor is most skilled at dealing with conscious material, and indeed, is on safer ground in doing so. Explorations of the subconscious are often best left to the psychiatrist, clinical social worker, or the psychologist. Many parishioners, however, can benefit greatly by learning new methods of living more functional lives.

Compassion, by itself, is not enough-although it is a good beginning. The compassionate, ethical pastor must care enough to become skilled. Caring and competency must go together.

Chapter 6

Behavioral Treatment

One of the painful symptoms and side effects of depression is the diminution of energy. When depression begins to affect the body with decreased energy, the individual feels less urge to attend meetings, to go to social events, to enter into physical or sexual contact with his or her spouse. The appetite decreases and the depressed person does what any of us would do under these circumstances—withdraws.

THE ENERGY CYCLE

At this point, a malignant cycle begins. The depressed persons feel bad and have little energy. They begin to reduce their number of appointments and activities. As they decrease their involvement in life, their personal and social reinforcement is reduced and they feel still less energy. First comes the loss of energy, then it is followed by diminished activities, which is followed by reduced rewards, which creates still less energy. The cycle continues until the depressed person attempts to withdraw completely from life. Even routine activities such as eating, bathing, and dressing become extremely difficult.

Thus, depression begins to reinforce itself through withdrawal and inactivity. One way to begin to reverse depression is to reverse this activity cycle.

There is a little known and understood relationship between brain chemistry and physical activity. We do know that certain brain chemicals in the form of neurotransmitters and hormones are stimulated by activity and exercise. For instance, the brain creates its own pleasure chemical in the form of endorphins—endogenous beta morphines. When we do not exercise, the brain has very little signal to produce this pleasurable sensation through endorphins. Most of us have heard of the runner's high, that sense of euphoria experienced by many athletes during physical exertion. Evidence points to the possibility of creating pleasurable sensations through physical activity.

Withdrawal and lethargy certainly tend to make a depression worse. The more activity we can comfortably encourage on the part of depressed people, the more likely we are to reverse the downward cycle of the depression.

Reengagement

Here the pastor can play a unique role in slowly and diplomatically reengaging the depressed person back into life. This must be done with extreme sensitivity and always with the awareness of the feelings of the parishioner. Pushed too rapidly, he or she will withdraw even more. Handled with the individual and his or her family in a diplomatic and pastoral way, reengagement on a gradual basis can be of great benefit in reintroducing pleasurable response to the depressed person's life.

Yoking

Another method in addition to reengagement is that of "yoking." This involves carefully finding and selecting a partner to assist the depressed person on a regular basis in performing routine activities that the withdrawn parishioner may not complete or be able to do on his own.

For example, the simple exercise of walking three times a week can work wonders in changing dysphoric moods. The yoke partner must be sensitive and caring enough to gently prod his friend into an agreed-upon exercise, even when the partner happens to not feel like doing so on any specified day. Certainly, this may be a tedious and even boring task unless the beneficial results can be kept in mind as the goal. Exercise maintains the cardiovascular system as well as producing healthy neurochemicals.

There are four major areas of behavioral (action) therapy to be explored here. Technically and theoretically speaking, any action, movement, or behavior that is used intentionally to make a person feel better falls into the category of behavior therapy. Not all action is curative or healing, but it may be used to determine what steps are efficacious and what ones are not. Here, we will limit ourselves to four areas. Certainly, there is an overlap with cognitive therapy. That is why this field is most often spoken of as cognitive-behavioral therapy.

PROBLEM SOLVING

This is a cognitive skill that leads to action and change. Often the depressed person has been or becomes overwhelmed with his or her inability to solve problems in daily life. Because of this skill deficit, problems or dilemmas mount until they become what seems to be an overwhelming and insurmountable complex set of issues. At this point, the pastor becomes a teacher, and strives to introduce simple, methodical steps in order to reduce a problem to a manageable size.

Few people, aside from a pastor, have access to both areas of action and thinking. The first principle in any problem-solving effort is to reduce the issue to one clear, specific difficulty. In other words, define the problem.

Many times, people will tangle so many issues together that their global complaints are difficult to decipher into one concrete issue. The pastor, priest, or rabbi can gently assist the parishioner in determining whether there really is a problem or not. A problem is defined as "a question proposed for solution, a knotty point to be cleared up."[1] The important thing here is to recognize that a problem has a solution; reality does not necessarily fall into that category. In other words, if the issue can be clearly stated and the problem defined, it may have a solution. On the other hand, if there is no known or available solution, we may be faced with a reality to be accepted.

This is a sticking point with many people. It is often difficult to understand the difference between reality and a problem.

After the first step is taken and the problem is defined in simple terms, the next stage is to look for possible answers. Sometimes this involves bringing in additional information or seeking additional help and advice from family, friends, or experts. The parishioner, however, should be encouraged to reduce the utilization of external help where possible and seek the resources within himself. Dependency should not be encouraged where the parishioner is capable of finding a solution or taking the next step by himself. The helpless/hopeless plea should be listened to only when reality suggests that there is no other answer or resource within the person.

After stage two is accomplished, a list of possible solutions should be written out and reviewed. Any action that is harmful to self or others should be eliminated. For example, if the person has unfinished business with a relationship such as a colleague or an associate, it might become harmful to express that directly. This may be better accomplished by writing a letter stating all of the negative feelings, and then reading this letter to the counselor. At that point (the third stage), the letter can be destroyed without hurting someone else, yet the same benefit is obtained. At this point, the most plausible action can be chosen and reviewed with the pastor. Remember, the parishioner has to make his or her own choices.

The fourth stage involves determining when the chosen action will be taken and what help will be needed in order to accomplish that action. A definite time and date will be determined and scheduled. When the most plausible solution is chosen and acted upon, the results should be reviewed again, preferably with paper and pencil. The action should be used as an experiment much as a scientist would use trial and error to clarify his or her hypotheses.

If an attempt at a solution fails the first or second time, this does not mean that there is a failure to solve the problem. This only indicates that one way has been tried and found to be unsuccessful. The pastor and parishioner are therefore freed to explore other possible solutions. If the attempt to solve the problem has proved successful, the depressed person can be taught to accept positive feelings (strokes) for having done most of the work herself. If it is an unsuccessful experiment, the parishioner can be shown that the method was unsuccessful, and that she needs to continue in the same direction until an appropriate solution is found.

Remember, there is no professional more suited to help struggling persons than the well-trained pastor. If the dilemma involves a difficulty that is inescapable yet painful, then with religious courage and faith, we must assist depressed persons in facing that reality. It often takes an ample dose of grace until we can move into true acceptance of indigestible situations.

After the above steps have been taken, and all the obvious solutions reviewed and found to be wanting, the problem must be restated in different terms and new trial solutions determined. The main point here is teaching the person how to clarify his problems and choose the method to use in solving them. When that is done, the parishioner must be helped and at times, forced into realizing that he has done a good job in solving his own situation. His strengths have led to competency and potency, and he must be assisted in accepting positive qualities about himself. This seems a minor point, yet one that most depressed persons need help to accomplish. Their negative view of themselves needs to be countered slowly with awareness of personal strengths, minor and major.

It may seem no big issue to give yourself strokes for taking a shower or balancing the checkbook, but let me assure you, the depressed person needs to reinforce all positive aspects about himself.

TIMING

Two parents took a little boy to his first symphony concert. He became fascinated with the musician who played the cymbals and thought it would be great fun to be able to grow up and clang the cymbals like he did. After the performance the parents took the little boy backstage where he talked with his favorite hero, the cymbal player. He asked the musician, "What do you have to know in order to play the cymbals?" This was a tough question. The musician thoughtfully considered the sincere query from the little boy. After a few moments he slowly said, "The one thing you must know is when."

I recently watched a group of very athletic acrobats practice their physically stressing and difficult routine. As they flew through the air, many feet above the crowd, their precision was awe inspiring. Their performances, and indeed their very lives, depended on learning how to trust each other and learning when to let go of one set of bars or trapezes and to reach out and grasp another. Timing became all important. So it is in pastoral counseling. We must learn when to trust another's strength, when to hold back, and when to let go and reach out for new security and growth.

Qualified counselors, pastoral or secular, must listen with their third ear and use all of their intuitive skills to determine "when."

PLEASANT EVENTS REINFORCEMENT

Through extensive research, Peter Lewinsohn has developed his therapeutic approach to depression control by means of behavioral change. Social learning theory would suggest that depression itself is learned. "Some individuals learn to act, think, and feel in depressing ways."[2]

We act differently in different situations. When we anticipate a certain event, we act according to our expectations. For example, in certain traffic areas, we anticipate patrol cars and govern our driving and behavior accordingly. In a formal setting with professional colleagues, we put on our intellectual demeanor, a mask we present to our peers or associates. We act with dignity and reserve.

It is a gift of grace to have a few friends or family members with whom we can be ourselves—no professional masks, no need to impress or to fake who or where we are at this moment of our lives. However, most of us would admit that we often change our behavior, even our clothes, and our countenance based upon anticipation of the situation about to confront us. Anticipation of situations, events, or people affects and guides our behavior.

Second, the results of a behavior (the consequence) influence its repetition or extinction. All behavior has consequences. These consequences—rewards or punishment—help to determine the frequency of the elimination (extinction) of the behavior. Behavior gets reinforced in subtle ways. Lewinsohn uses this example about "payoffs" to illustrate the point.

Holly's parents are very important people in their community. They care very much for Holly, but because of their active schedules, they haven't been able to spend much time with her. She had always understood and even shared in their roles as community leaders, but there was something nice about how they took more time to be with her when she looked sad and troubled.

Holly didn't feel sad frequently, but when she did, she was able to have warm heart-to-heart talks with her parents.

Holly became worried when she began to have periods of sadness more often than before. At first she wondered whether it was just that she was getting older and her worries were more serious, but somehow this explanation was not satisfactory. At the suggestion from a friend of the family, Holly asked her parents to set aside a certain amount of time for her each week, at a regular time. The sad periods became less frequent.

What the friend had noticed was that, without intentionally doing so, Holly's parents were teaching her to become sad. They were providing positive consequences each time Holly felt bad and showed it by her depressed expression. The irony in the situation was that, even with the best of intentions, her parents were training Holly to become sad to get attention.[3]

If a behavior is positively reinforced (rewarded), it is then likely that behavior will be repeated frequently. If the consequences are negative (painful, aversive), then that behavior will likely be repeated less often or eventually be extinguished. Ignoring a behavior will usually lead to the extinction and eradication of that behavior.

If a behavior is consistently ignored, the subject will discontinue that unrewarding and unrewarded activity. If however, the actions are responded to sporadically, it becomes very difficult to extinguish that behavior. Behavior that is intermittently reinforced is the most difficult to extinguish.

All behavior has a payoff; otherwise, we do not expend the energy necessary to act. Depression itself has rewards and punishments. While punishment may appear negative on the surface, it can often accomplish the unconscious goal of gaining attention. Even negative attention is better than none.

Likewise, depression may elicit sympathy, concern, worry, affection, and care from the surrounding audience of family, friends, colleagues, and health professionals. Certainly, much of this can be on an unconscious or subconscious level, but nonetheless, real and powerful.

Feelings (emotions), actions (behavior), and thought process (cognition) are all interrelated. We might add a fourth estate and point out that our body (physical being) is profoundly related to our thoughts, actions, and emotions. We may be happy or sad, energetic or lethargic, based upon our physical (bodily) well-being. Even faith and trust are related to hormonal and chemical balances in our bodies.

Learning theories indicate that thoughts, actions, feelings, and physical condition continually influence each other in a nonending interaction of body-mind-spirit.

Therefore, learning theory helps us understand why we have felt and behaved in such a way. It also helps us develop treatment strategies to change the way we feel and direct our behavior in the future.

Self-change is difficult. It requires more than brute will (or won't) power. Good intentions are not sufficient. Contracted agreements that provide rewards and punishments become necessary to insure completion of chosen behavior. Contractual agreements should be specific, time limited, and precise in specifying behavior desired. Avoid global and general goals.

Rewards have at least four requirements:

1. They must be something chosen specifically as a positive and pleasant event.
2. They must be accessible to the subject.
3. They must have sufficient strength or intensity to adequately reward for time and effort expended.
4. They must be something you can control.[4]

Delayed reward or gratification tends to have minimal strength as a positive or negative reinforcer. The closer the behavior is to the consequence, the more power the latter carries to influence future behavior.

THE PAIN-PLEASURE CONTINUUM

Lewinsohn[5] has developed an excellent Pleasant Events Schedule, which he uses with his clients. It lists some 320 items that are to be rated as to frequency and degree of pleasure. From this list, one may develop an understanding of the events which engender some response and those which are rated either neutral or negative. By reinforcing the items that elicit a positive response, the individual, with the guidance of the pastor, is enabled to enhance the pleasurable aspects of his or her life. The actual scheduling of rewarding situations combats the anhedonia (loss of pleasure), rewards positive action, and helps return the parishioner to a more active role in life. By so doing, the person may actually lift some of the depression and hopefully alter the neurotransmitter balance in the brain.

Pastors may greatly assist parishioners in developing their own pleasant events schedule. This can be time consuming and tedious, but the rewards may prove to be worth the effort. This also provides an opportunity for the parishioners to have objective homework assignments that will help them regain the sense of control over their moods.

The more positive, objective steps of this nature, the more that potentiation can take place. Remember, the goal of developing a reinforcement schedule of pleasurable events must become the parishioner's goal; objectives must be clear with agreed upon time lines.

First, the regular activities of the day should be listed. Most depressives will claim they get little reward from brushing their teeth, taking a shower, getting up at an agreed upon time, or keeping appointments. They should be assisted in charting this routine behavior and hopefully be led to accept some positive feeling from being able to complete these routine procedures.

Second, time should be spent in developing those things which are appropriate and truly pleasant or rewarding to the depressed person. What is "pleasurable" for one person is not necessarily meaningful to the next. Spend enough time with the person to get them to describe what makes joy in their lives.

Next, rewarding activities should be scheduled and completed as a religious obligation to the self. Most depressives tend to downplay that which is pleasurable. They seem to have been taught that duty and responsibility come before anything else in life, and that if they enjoy something, it must be wrong. A thorough misunderstanding of Calvinism has put a damper on pleasure for many sincerely religious people. We need to not only learn to schedule our stress but to also schedule rewarding, renewing, and recreating moments in life. The better job we do of this, the more we will move away from the pain of depression to the awareness of joy and happiness.

Do not take this part of behavior therapy flippantly or lightly. Remember, changing our behavior can alter our moods.

POSITIVE ASSERTIVENESS TRAINING

The United Nations, under the leadership of Eleanor Roosevelt and others, spent many agonizing hours of deliberation, debate, study, and disagreement before arriving at what has come to be a profound statement of universal human rights. These rights are to be sought after as ideals, hopes, and dreams that someday can be guaranteed to all humanity. Paul of Tarsus had such a dream, which he captured from his revelation through Christ. No longer would there be Jew or Gentile, enslaved or free. Men, women, children—people of all races, colors, and ethnic and national backgrounds—would enjoy the privileges set forth in this statement. The Declaration of Universal Human Rights belongs with such great documents as the Magna Carta, the Declaration of Independence, and the Constitution of The United States. Listen beyond the words to some of the deeply embedded hopes for all humankind.

Most persons of the Judeo-Christian tradition, and certainly many others of different faiths, including scientific and humanistic, would firmly endorse a value system where the dignity and worth of the individual is upheld and affirmed. As one author proclaimed, "I believe that man will not merely endure: he will prevail."[6] Therefore, if we can acknowledge these rights, privileges, and prerogatives for others, can we not affirm them for ourselves? The entire assertiveness training movement is about allowing and assisting human beings to affirm who and what they are.

In 1977, Patricia Palmer wrote a children's book entitled *The Mouse, The Monster, and Me.* This was preceded and followed by a number of books and courses designed to help people become pleasantly assertive (maintain their own dignity) without resorting to either submissiveness and passivity (the mouse), or the aggressive, obnoxious bully who domineers, controls and manipulates, either by force or emotional coercion (the monster).

In many cases of marriage counseling, it has become evident that the husband has to learn assertiveness skills. Likewise, the wife, but from a different angle, has to learn similar skills to avoid becoming passive-aggressive or seeking to get her needs met through subversion. The relevance for the treatment of depression becomes obvious when we realize and accept the fact that depressed people have the right to expect certain treatment with dignity and to teach their friends and family how to treat them honestly.

There are excellent resources available. Pastors have the opportunity, if not the responsibility, to teach people in their congregation how to communicate their needs, wants, and desires with honest communication. Once this is learned, life becomes a matter of helping each other meet the highest potential of which we are capable.[7]

RELAXATION TRAINING

Several years ago, we in the mental health center were asked to work with a young woman in her early thirties who suffered from problems of anxiety and insomnia. After several counseling sessions, it became obvious that she could benefit from some relaxation training procedures. After being instructed in the office in both progressive and passive procedures, she was loaned a tape to use during the day and at bedtime. We selected a commercial tape prepared by a very competent and professional specialist. She left rather eager to get on with her practice. The next morning, after our office opened, this normally feisty but pleasant woman came storming into our office and threw the tape down on the secretary's desk, declaring that she wouldn't listen to it. Her statement was, "I am not about to let any man tell me what to do." Apparently, she did not want to take instruction from a male, although her counselor had been a male. She was then given a tape with a woman's voice and later helped in making a tape of her own voice.

Everyone has a different style and method of handling stress. We relax in different ways, and what is helpful to one person is not necessarily helpful to another. One psychologist unwinds by lying on the floor and listening to thirty minutes of Mozart. Another woman finds her solace in private time at her organ. As pastoral counselors, we can assist individuals in handling their stress in constructive ways.

Where humanly possible, there are a few rules that must be followed. First, there must be a firm recognition of the importance of releasing and reducing our inner stress. Second, there must be a genuine commitment to take the necessary steps to restore body, mind, and soul on a regular basis. Third, a fixed time must be scheduled as an obligation to fulfill to ourselves and our future well-being. Fourth, a quiet place must be designated and kept as inviolate as possible, to be used each day for the purpose of prayer, meditation, relaxation, biofeedback, autogenic phrases, comforting music, or whatever other techniques are workable for that individual.

Remember, stress management or relaxation training must be individualized.

One method that I use is the set of autogenic phrases developed by the Menninger Foundation. These statements or "self-talk" have proven very effective in helping people relax and learn how to relieve tension. Life Sciences Institute of Mind-Body Health in Topeka is an outgrowth of one of the projects of the Menninger Clinic. Dr. Steven Fahrion and others on the staff are very knowledgeable in the field of biofeedback and stress reduction, and have proven extremely helpful to pastors and counselors helping their parishioners find release from tension. The individual can use these (or other) affirmations for several days, and if proven helpful, can record these in his or her own voice. There are many excellent guidelines available through public libraries, psychological publishing houses, and bookstores. Do not be afraid to experiment with different methods until the right one is found for you or the person you are assisting.

The only basic security any of us have is grounded in God, the ultimate reality of the universe. Whether we approach that God through Christ, faith, mysticism, or even our rational minds, our souls do not and cannot find true relief and release except in and through the integration of ourselves with the universe of which we are a part.

Chapter 7

The Pastor: Unique Caregiver

The model for the competent and skilled pastor is now and always has been Christ, the author and guide for our faith and our profession. As Christ modeled His ministry on the Hebrew Scriptures, which included the law and the teachings of the prophets, as well as the oral traditions of the Hebrew faith, the pastor should be knowledgeable of the wisdom contained in this profound religious faith. The acquaintanceship must go beyond simply knowing what this material contains. It must include deep understanding in the pastor's mind and conscience until the spirit, the intent, can be grasped. The meaning of the Scriptures must be brought into the modern world, where the letter of the law cannot be applied to the modern technological era. The "spirit" can revitalize and invigorate, where the letter is obsolescent and stilted.

I remember an old saying of unknown origin that went something like this:

The meanest man I ever saw,
always stayed within the law.

So is it often with the use or misuse of Scripture. It is incumbent upon us to struggle—to wrestle—with the Scriptures and our traditions until we catch a glimpse of the meaning, the spirit, the dynamic behind and within them. There are immense changes in technology, medical science, philosophy, and mathematics that make it difficult to transpose these into the ethos of "the biblical era." While the specifics may be obsolete, the spirit, the will, the intent of the Scriptures and its authors remain as vital today as ever before. Perhaps modern psychology has enabled us to put into practice the commandment to love God and our neighbors as ourselves.

The pastor must face the reality of the existence of mental illness. Many pastors raised in a naive and progressive liberal era would like to believe that mental illness will evaporate and go away. The psychology of success often becomes the theology of success achievement. If the parishioner will apply biblical principles, he or she will then be the exemplar of the successful and affluent American businessperson: healthy, wealthy, and wise.

Therefore, when emotional disturbance disrupts a marriage, a family, or an individual's life, the pastor may interpret this as an anomaly best left to the medical profession. Mental illness exists. It is an entity that must be faced and dealt with as a real-life problem to be reconciled along with our other concepts of physical illness.

Fairchild (1980)[1] points to the words of a psychiatrist to legitimize the work of the pastor:

No psychiatrists or psychotherapists, even those with many patients, have the quantitive numerous opportunities to cure souls and mend minds, which the preacher enjoys. And the preacher also has a superb opportunity to do what few psychiatrists can, to prevent the development of chronic anxiety, depression, and other mental ills.

Some physical illness is biological in nature. It may be "caused" by faulty heredity, influenced by malnutrition, absorbed through interaction with the environment, or precipitated by physical injury and/or emotional trauma. Physical illness may have a complex structure of causality. The origin of gall bladder disease becomes of interest only in the name of treatment and prevention. If we understand what causes or triggers certain problems, we may be able to prevent them and treat them more intelligently. So it is with mental illness. The root causes are of interest in the name of prevention and treatment. In the face of a suffering parishioner, the focus is not upon etiology but upon remediation: easing the pain and pointing out changes that may lessen the course of suffering. Pastors, of all professionals, are those who may assume a certain amount of the suffering upon themselves, and walk with parishioners in times of illness.

Evil exists. Even if we describe illness as the absence of health, or evil as the absence of goodness, we still must deal with the ever-present reality of unspeakable pain in the world. We must seek to be part of the healing rather than a part of the judgmental condemnation that contributes to this pain. War is hell. So is mental illness. Let us confront the fact that the pastor, adequately trained and skilled, may fill a role that does not and cannot fit any other professional.

Ministers have many roles that they must play. If a minister is appointed to a parish, the front line of religious faith, then he or she must be preacher, teacher, cheerleader, business manager, program director, prophet, family friend, bearer of values, judge, community spokesman, and the trained professional Christian within their geographical area. The smaller the population and the more expanded the geographic territory, the more these roles become necessary to assume. In a large urban church, the senior pastor (I dislike that term—one is either the pastor or not) may delegate some of these roles to others on the staff or to professionals within the community. The farther from metropolitan areas and the more sparsely spaced the parishioners are, the more of these roles the minister must assume. Some ministers have the luxury of assuming the portfolio for preaching. They become focused on their pulpit performance at specific times designated by their denominations and perhaps their own choices. Some specialists avoid preaching and leave that to the more vocal associate. There are ministers for education, for pastoral home and hospital visitation, for programming, for youth, and for administration. They may delegate responsibility for the care of souls to others they deem more qualified or willing to assume that task.

It is difficult to understand how a minister can preach to the needs of human beings without walking the same paths that they must walk. To be a powerful bearer of the good news of and from God, one must walk humbly and closely with those given to his charge.

The pastor is more than a therapist. This in no way is intended to be a delimiting statement about secular therapists. There are many competent and sincere psychiatrists, psychologists, social workers, well-trained counselors, internists, and family physicians. Each of them carries his or her own bundle of beliefs. Each has his or her own faith—part good, part bad. But it is only the pastor that can fulfill certain therapeutic functions not available to anyone else.

Seward Hiltner[2] discusses the functions of the minister through the idea of images (roles) and delineates nine such activities to be performed. These interrelated yet separate functions are:

1. preaching
2. teaching
3. theologizing
4. administering
5. evangelizing
6. celebrating
7. reconciling
8. disciplining
9. shepherding

Each function is related to a unified whole: the ministry. As such, they are units that go together to comprise the role set of the complex and sometimes ambiguous professional picture. Some are better qualified by training and temperament to perform one activity better than another. One person cannot be expected to be adequately equipped, nor personally suited, to excel in all of them.[3]

Samuel C. Webb[4] reviewed much of the literature on church-related vocations, especially the Protestant ministry, and discovered an amazing array of roles to be studied. Thirty suggested roles were selected for examination by factor analysis. On the basis of this method, sixteen factors could be identified as roles. They were: administrator, student-scholar, spiritual guide and example, counselor, therapist, social reformer, church musician, preacher, evangelist, denominational representative, public speaker, teacher, priest, maintainer of status quo, writer, and group fellowship leader.

After further study, it was decided that the maintainer of status quo and group fellowship leader roles be dropped. The roles of counselor-therapist, preacher-speaker, and scholar-writer were combined. After further experimental use of subjects from theological schools across the country, ten scales were adopted as delineating the major roles of clergymen. These roles were: counselor, administrator, teacher, scholar, evangelist, spiritual guide, preacher, reformer, priest, and musician.

Perhaps the most extensive research ever made of the Protestant ministry was underwritten by the Danforth Foundation and published as the two-volume work by Kenneth Underwood.[5] Underwood recognized four major functions of the minister that must be kept in balance to provide a whole ministry. These four areas of service are the following:

1. *The Pastoral Role:* That of caring for individuals within a religious context
2. *The Priestly Role:* That of proclaiming the faith and its gospel and of carrying out the ritual acts that affirm the central tenets of that faith
3. *The Prophetic Role:* That of judging the justice and humanity of the social order and pointing to the changes required if these values are to be present
4. *The Kingly Role:* That of governance and organization of activities for the care of men in the world through corporate (responsible) action

These four roles—pastoral, priestly, prophetic, and governance—become dominant functions to be understood, examined, and performed by the well-rounded minister. It is the pastoral role, that of the shepherd of souls, that becomes the focus of our attention in the healing of clinical depression.

Psychiatrist Edgar Draper points out that the minister or professional representative of a religious faith must take upon himself the power and authority of his role and its significance. Many pastoral counselors and/or pastors seek to become amateur psychiatrists or psychologists. They neglect, if not denigrate, their function as a religious professional, without apology. "Our concept of pastoral care begs the clergyman to reappreciate the potential of religious resources, besides counseling, to meet human needs."[6]

Draper expresses his concern that ministers will neglect the unique role given to them and therefore leave a void in the cluster of healing specialties.

Should pastoral counseling be called and function as a "specialty" of the ministry? Is it, like church music or religious education, a field of interest familiar to most practicing pastors and a specific vocation of the few? (1) How does pastoral counseling differ from psychotherapy? (2) If there are differences, are these simply nominal, hiding therapeutic maneuvers behind the aegis of religion? (3) If differences are real, what are the specific contributions to be made by the pastoral counselor? (4) If differences are nominal, does the training or the pastoral counselor meet secular psychotherapeutic standards? (5) What are the qualifications for a recognized pastoral counselor, and do these reflect the training background or experience that carries weight in the psychological helping professions?[7]

As a broad and tentative definition, a pastoral counselor is a therapist who by design, intent, and commitment is a pastor. This would raise red flags about the specialty of "pastoral counselor" when it is divorced from the church or from the role of minister or pastor. The pastoral counselor is first a pastor who is committed and trained to be a shepherd of souls.

Many questions are raised about definitions of therapy, theology, and pastoral counseling, which are better left to other studies. An individual's ordination is a license to counsel. The question then becomes one of whether we counsel wisely or poorly, competently or haphazardly. In areas of uncertainty, the responsible pastor must seek assistance and become competent to deal with the human issues that confront him or her.

Several years ago, I was called upon to administer the sacraments and provide other religious services to a patient in the hospital who was suffering from what is commonly called a nervous breakdown. The psychiatrist stated that he had gone as far as he could in psychotherapy with this person, but that a pastor could provide therapeutic techniques and resources that medical science did not (and perhaps could not) utilize. Through the sharing of communion, Scripture, and prayer, the woman was able to access deeper levels of her psyche and begin the profound healing profess.

There is a place for the pastor and priest in healing. It cannot be left entirely to the medical or psychological professions. The caveat here, however, is for conscientious ministers to bring to bear not only their wealth of religious background and values, but to combine their compassion and deep love of human beings with the competency and skill of modern psychological wisdom.

The parishioner very seldom "sees" the pastor as he or she really is, instead considering him or her only in terms of earlier images and relationships. This distortion of current reality is a normal occurrence in everyday relationships and is heightened in the pastoral or therapeutic setting.

Most clinically trained clergy are taught to read the human documents before them: they seek to understand the inner world of the parishioner in order to empathize with his or her dilemmas, dreams, and hopes. In "reading" or understanding this human document, we become aware that the parishioner sees us in roles, both good and bad, that we may or may not deserve.

An injunction by a chaplain supervisor in the Texas Medical Center was to realize that pastors in training were seen by ill patients as the representative (if not the image) of God. What a terrifying insight! Nevertheless, pastors must assume with fear and trembling this expectation placed upon them. It becomes imperative at some point in the therapeutic relationship to clarify this expectation. In the meantime, the skilled pastoral therapist must learn to use this positive transference in a wholesome way. In essence, the patient or parishioner is giving us power to help them grow toward health and wholeness.

The mantle of religious authority is one often abused or misused. When any of us accept the fact that people do not see us as we are, we may begin to learn how to utilize this positive or negative transference in a significant way.

There are dangers in this role of being a surrogate for God, or a vicar of Christ, in assuming the mantle of religious authority. With the mantle comes the obligation of restraint, humility, and wisdom. Let us use our power wisely; but let us use it.

The second caveat to pastoral counselors, as well as to psychiatrists and psychologists, is to beware of violating the first commandment. When we get in touch with our power and what measure of competence we might have, let us not assume that we can "heal" all the ills, or be all things to all persons. In the final analysis, healing is a gift of God. The healer simply assists in removing the barriers to the healing process. Remember, simple does not mean easy.

Pastors, as value bearers, carry with them the weight of ecclesiastic tradition, the vast and rich history of the people, the resource of the written word, and the collective strength of their congregation. These strengths are a gift to pastors, which they assume by virtue of their office. Modern pastors should become aware of all the resources that are given to them, and learn to use them in service of healing depressed people.

Several decades ago, there was a fellowship group from both Protestant and Catholic traditions that called itself the Yokefellows. They believed that to enter into a commitment with a depressed person was to willingly accept certain responsibilities in assisting others in areas in which they cannot assist themselves. It is neither a permanent nor even a long-term situation, but a temporary contractual commitment to assist in the healing process. For example, it has been found helpful to walk two to three miles a day, three times a week. If the parishioner does not demonstrate enough emotional or physical strength to do this on her own, a partner is enlisted who will agree to covenant with the parishioner and fulfill this exercise with her until she is able to do it by herself. Yoking can be a powerful tool at the command of the pastor, and was discussed in Chapter 6.

Pastors have a unique relationship with the family of the depressed person. Pastors become interpreters of what is occurring in the illness, what treatment is being applied, and the necessity of the family's cooperation with helping professionals in the healing process. Families may either enhance therapy or be a major obstacle in helping the sick person become well. Pastors may use their office in guiding the family in their assistance and cooperation.

Always remember the ethical imperative of confidentiality. When maintaining the relationship between family and patient, always be careful not to reveal any aspects that are confidential in nature. Pastors may lose whatever credibility they have by volunteering information that the parishioner or counselor has shared with them in trust. When in doubt, be quiet.

Like it or not, the pastor is often called upon to be a social worker—the reliever of social/familial stresses. This category is assumed more by default, i.e., there are no other persons to fill this role. Sometimes housing, clothing, food, or employment play a significant role in current stressors. With the assistance of the relevant members of the congregation, the pastor may seek to alleviate some of these problems, where other personnel are not available.

Under the unique role of pastor, there are three areas that seem to be of utmost pastoral sensitivity. The pastor can be:

1. A transformer of victimhood;
2. An encourager and enabler of risk taking; or
3. A guide to logotherapy.

Depressed people often adopt a victim role in society and relationships. We often hear, "Why me? I always have the bad luck." Another will say, "I feel helpless," or "Life is a cruel joke and I always wind up as the joke." Such thinly disguised self-pity is genuinely felt and should be accepted as sincere. There is no other professional as equipped as the theologian/pastor to lead a depressed person gently from victimhood to victor. The apostle Paul often wrote in his epistles to early churches about how he learned to be more than a conqueror in the face of many negative and degrading situations. This power of the transformation from victimhood to victor is given to us. Let us share it gently with the suffering parishioner.

Second, the pastor may encourage new behavior on the part of the patient. When a person is depressed, he or she usually retreats to a safe routine or regresses to earlier, more helpless states upon which he or she was dependent during infancy or childhood. With gentle prodding and sensitive leading, we can assist wounded people to slowly assume more and more independence, and to extend their current repertoire of behavior and reaction to new expressions of life and wholeness. People can learn to direct their moods and emotions. It is the pastor's task to assist in that growth.

Jesus encouraged His disciples to get out of the boat and try something new. Where retribution was the habitual response to insult, He taught forgiveness. Where anger or indifference was the order of the day, Jesus counseled His disciples to learn to love. Can we do any less?

Third, the pastor is the primary professional in the area of logotherapy. Logotherapy is a form of healing that became highlighted with the writings of Victor Frankl, A.J. Ungersma, and others. It developed during World War II, a time when the entire world was insane with hatred, murder, cruelty, barbarism, and unspeakable horror.

Frankl said he could survive this brutality only if he could find meaning within it. To paraphrase both Frankl and Nietzsche, a person will find a "how to live" if he can find a "why to live."

The heroic struggle of many to survive concentration camps brought hope and meaning—likewise with depressive episodes, if meaning can be found within them. We then not only survive the episodes, but prevail over them.

Some conscientious pastors have a tendency to take on more responsibility than they can handle or more than they are trained or equipped to handle. Pastors should closely examine themselves at this point and see if they have this tendency. Strive to share some of the tasks better done by someone else. Often, it is our own insecurity or grandiosity (the Jehovah complex) that pulls us in that direction. For the sake of others, and ourselves, let us define our tasks and goals and be generous in our sharing (not shirking) of responsibility.

Chapter 8

A Theology of Pastoral Care

Any serious consideration of pastoral counseling for and with people who are depressed must take into account the foundational theology of the pastor, both implicit and explicit. It is often the hidden premises out of which we operate that create obstacles or barriers to our verbal and nonverbal communications. For example, if one assumes that this life is a veil of tears and only a temporary trial to prepare us "for a better place," then he or she does not place considerable emphasis on the quality of this life, nor does the person expect certain types of fulfillment or satisfaction. Indeed, early orthodoxy and later fundamentalism approached this life as full of suffering and pain, and that it was intended to be so. Naive liberalism later began to approach this life as heaven on earth with fulfillment of all our desires, needs, and wishes. Certainly the optimistic periods of growth and development within the United States during the 1940s and 1950s not only expected a chicken in every pot and a car in every garage, but health, prosperity, and happiness on a universal scale.

That such assumptions were not seriously questioned after World War I or World War II led to bitter confusion and disillusionment. The outgrowth of neoorthodoxy and pessimism led one to believe that humanity could control very little of its environment or cosmic habitation. Nor could it confront its intrapsychic problems or interpersonal social dilemmas realistically and with hope.

Some educators indicated that there were only two basic types of philosophy: that of pessimism and that of optimism. Albert Camus attempted to condense all of philosophy and theology by oversimplifying the basic question as being whether or not to commit suicide. A humbling experience of examining our deep-rooted convictions about life, death, eternity, and meaning of existence will not only clarify our assumptions but perhaps engender some overdue intellectual humility. *Solid faith is always built on struggle, and must ever be so.* Like Jacob wrestling with the angel, we must wrestle with our own angels and demons in order to stand in awe and wonder at the marvels and miracles of human existence.

The true mark of educated people is not their degrees, but their intellectual humility. As one scientist said, the one thing incomprehensible about the universe is that it is comprehensible. The mind of man cannot know all things, but can know some things. The mind that can grasp the universe is no less amazing than the universe that it grasps.

GOD VIEW

One little girl was drawing a picture with crayons when her teacher walked by and asked her what she was doing. The little girl stated with self-assurance that she was drawing a picture of God. The teacher was amused and taken aback. She told the little girl that no one knows what God looks like, to which the little girl calmly replied: "They will when I am finished."

Our images or lack of images about God come from long forgotten roots in our subconscious. Jung would perhaps suggest that they may come from our collective unconscious, that is, our unconscious, embedded memories of the human race. Certainly, our first ideas about God are learned from our parents, our siblings and society, our churches and their traditions, our own human reasoning, and our composite collection of experiences.

Several years ago, I took an informal survey of boys in a federal correctional facility. This research sought to determine the correlation, if any, between the nature and predisposition of the father in the home, and the boys' concept of God. It was an amateurish and informal study, yet it quickly revealed that many of the boys who had no father in the home had no God concept. From their perspective, God was absent from and uninvolved in the universe and the world of personal experience.

Similarly, boys who had a vindictive and punitive, even abusive, father thought of God in judgmental and angry terms. An alcoholic father would often produce a son who thought of God as capricious, undependable, and punishing.

The interesting part of this study for me was that I found no boys in the correctional facility that had "good fathers," i.e., fathers that were in the home, who held down regular jobs, and who placed the welfare of their families uppermost in their daily lives.

God, at least in the Western world, has been thought of largely in masculine terms. Therefore, the father has become the primary reference point by which judgments about God are to be measured. On a more subconscious level, the extent of healthy mothering influences the God concept positively or negatively.

As we examine our God concept(s), we will look at teachings from the church and the Bible, from tradition, from experience, and from reason. Tillich uses the reference of the "God beyond God." I believe what he means here is that our ideas never quite define or capture God. Even as we attempt to define God, we become increasingly aware of our difficulty in doing so. God is always more than our definition. So shall it ever be.

There was wisdom in the Hebrew usage of the tetragrammaton-JHVH (signifying the proper name of God). It could not be pronounced; it defied definition. Certainly, the Masoretes added vowels, and through the years, JHVH became Jahveh, then Jehovah. But in its original form, the tetragrammaton was undefinable and unspeakable. To define is to limit, and to limit is to lessen and desecrate. That is one reason for the emphasis on the commandment "Thou shalt not take the name of the Lord, thy G-d in vain." So, in pastoral care, as we attempt the urgent and significant task of building a workable definition and idea about God, let us keep in mind that we are always talking about our conceptions, our ideation about ultimate reality, or God, and that there is still much left out, ill-defined, or undefined. Nevertheless, the task must be approached.

GOD AS CREATOR

Perhaps we may seek to depersonalize this concept and think of God as the creative force within life and the cosmos. We must think in anthropomorphic terms, for those are the only tools we have as human beings. God, or ultimate reality (whatever that is), is the central factor of the universe out of which all other powers emerge. God created out of nothing—*creativo ex nihilo*—and in many theologies continues to create in the current epoch of history. In other words, God is not finished with creation, but is continuing "a new work" and will continue to do so.

This creative force is hopefully benevolent toward mankind and the individuals within that group. It would be difficult to worship or attempt to "love" a God that was not a benevolent, creative force. We might stand in awe of a different kind of God, but could not enter into a trust relationship in which hope was engendered. There are those that see God as an incomprehensible power that is to be feared and appeased rather than responded to in love and trust.

All pastors, counselors, psychologists, and psychiatrists need to periodically examine their basic assumptions about life, God, and the universe. This will allow them to become more genuine in their relationships with others and at least become conscious of obstacles to hope, faith, and genuineness.

CHRIST:
OUR TEACHER, EXAMPLE, AND REDEEMER

The sensitive ground of Christology is beyond the intent and scope of this book. The Christian church has dealt, even struggled, with trying to express beliefs centered around Jesus, the Christ. The early creeds were always testimonies of faith rather than an attempt to make them a test of faith as they later became. One of the simplest expressions deals with Jesus as teacher, example, and redeemer—the Savior of the world.

Jesus fulfilled the traditional task of the rabbi, albeit an uncertified or untrained one: that of being a teacher of the faith. Belief in God, for Christ, was simplified by referring to the Creator as "our heavenly father." Today, that language is less appropriate than it was. It has been accused of gender bias and discrimination. Jesus was a teacher who led by parable, reprimand, direction, and guidance. The role of teacher was implicit in what he was and what he did.

As an example, Jesus set the stage for his disciples of every generation to follow. Witness the woman at the well in Samaria, or the tax collector up the tree. The tax collectors must not have been any more popular then than they are now. Jesus in the Garden of Gethsemane became the model for prayer and personal communion with God. Jesus, by example, taught us much about compassion, mercy, service, humility, and nonjudgmental love.

He also modeled the role anger can play in righteous indignation in the face of corruption. He was not soft on the money changers nor did he coddle the Pharisees. Certainly, He was not afraid to take a stand, even if it meant persecution or punishment. He was accustomed to being rejected by others. Jesus became the example for Christians throughout the ages, and when we are functioning at our best, we are embodying the qualities He exemplified for us.

Redeemer

The dictionary defines a redeemer as one who redeems or buys back. To redeem is to ransom, buy back, to employ to the best purpose, to rescue, to atone for, or to perform what has been promised. Certainly, one of the main functions of a redeemer is to rescue or ransom that which has been lost, stolen, or forgotten. Jesus, the Christ, sought to buy back a lost generation or a confused people gone astray. He pointed out not only their potentials as human beings, but also shared what a true loving society could be like as people lived in relationship with a loving, caring God.

THE HOLY SPIRIT

Following the resurrection and ascension, the first disciples were overwhelmed with remorse at their unfaithfulness and a profound sense of abandonment in a threatening world. On the road to Emmaus and elsewhere, they became significantly aware that there was a presence among them that empowered their struggle. This spiritual presence became so real that the Apostles developed the concept of the Trinity, which was blasphemous to many. This suggested that God could be experienced as the creative force—God the Father—through Jesus Christ the Son, and through the abiding and indwelling presence, the Holy Spirit.

At the Institute for Advanced Pastoral Studies in Detroit, many pastors and members of other helping professions struggled personally and intellectually with the concept of the Holy Spirit and its actions in our lives. How can you grasp a wisp of air, or define a sunset, or describe the sense of wonder as you hold a newborn infant? So many of life's experiences are so large and profound that they can never be condensed into descriptions. In the old cliché, they defy definition. Yet, attempt to define we must.

The Holy Spirit can neither be commanded nor produced at will. It is a profound act of grace, a gift, that can come to us as individuals or within a group of individuals. It does not so much descend from above as it emerges from within. The Christian is instructed to prepare for this action of God, but is also enjoined against attempting to control or command it.

Let me try to illustrate. People may seek to reach a tangible goal that is important to them. Their task is to prepare the soil, plant the seed, weed the field, cultivate, and water and fertilize the plant. They cannot control, but may direct, influence, and enhance the final outcome. In the field of interpersonal relationships, this quality (the Holy Spirit) can operate after the conditions are provided for intimacy or growth to take place. The conditions may be established and the relationship of peace or intimacy not obtained. The desired results are not mechanical to conform to the known laws of physics or psychology. If the gift of peace or intimacy is reached, it is a gift of grace, the work of the Holy Spirit. It becomes imperative upon the Christian to do his or her homework, plow the field, and fulfill the conditions while seeking to be in tune with (at one with: atonement) that spirit which is called holy.

DOCTRINE OF THE INCARNATION

God was in Christ, reconciling the world unto himself. According to the Christian faith, God was in Christ, Immanuel, for the purpose of leading humanity back into a closer relationship with the creative God. The doctrine of the incarnation is far more significant, if that is possible, than simply shrugging off this concept with a statement that "God was in Christ." It must be taken further to indicate that God operates in and through the world through human flesh and spirit, with all of its weaknesses and strengths. If we are to know God, it may be that we cannot do so in the privacy of our closets, but rather through communication and communion with others. Martin Luther suggested the priesthood of all believers. He also said, "Go out and be Christ to someone today." What an awesome thought.

If God is a reality, a current presence in the contemporary world, we must then be able to point to that which is present in reality and be able, at least partially, to explain or illustrate what we mean. In the event of crises on a global scale, how does God operate? Does He, by fiat, solve the hunger in Somalia, or cause a change in the heart of a Saddam Hussein, or interrupt the riots in an inner city such as Los Angeles? Or does this creative benevolent power who is said to know each one of us by name (what a task) operate in and through His human creation to solve the problems of mankind?

If God wished to build shelter for homeless people, would He not do it through human hands? If God sought to heal a sick person, would it be wrong to think of it being done through a human representative (incarnation) of God? Would it be blasphemous to say that feeding the hungry is a task that God would endorse and accomplish not through supernatural means, but through human endeavor and compassion? The doctrine of the incarnation needs to be expanded to include, but not be limited to, the idea of God in each of us compelled into the world to accomplish and further the act, and indeed continuing the act or process of creation.

Kathryn Guthrie, a minister of the United Church of Canada, points out:

> The criteria, then, for assessing models and images of God that may be helpful to persons in recovery are these:
>
> 1. That the model reflect a belief that God is compassionate, loving, and gracious;
> 2. That the model reflect a belief that God is intimately involved in the struggle of human recovery and discovery of who one is and affirms human vulnerability;
> 3. That the model reflect a belief that God is a "power with," rather than a "power over"; and
> 4. That the model reflect a belief that God offers the possibility of real change and hope for a future different from the past and that human choices shape that difference.[1]

Scripture has been very helpful in that it enjoins us to always "test the spirit" to see if it be of God or not. A spirit that is mean, destructive, sadistic, or self-righteous comes not from Scripture or Christ, nor from God, but from the meanness and littleness still present in our world.

> Finally, my brethren, be strong in the Lord, and in the power of his might. Put on the whole armor of God, that you may be able to stand against the wiles of the devil. For we wrestle not against flesh and blood, but against principalities, against powers, against the rulers of the darkness of this world, against spiritual wickedness in high places. ... Stand therefore, having your loins girt about with truth, and having on the breastplate of righteousness; and your feet shod with the preparation of the gospel of peace; above all, taking the shield of faith, wherewith you shall be able to quench all the fiery darts of the wicked. And take the helmet of salvation, and the sword of the spirit, which is the word of God. (Ephesians 6:10-17)

> Finally, brethren, whatsoever things are true, whatsoever things are honest, whatsoever things are just, whatsoever things are pure, whatsoever things are lovely, whatsoever things are of good report; if there be any virtue, and if there be any praise, think on these things. (Philippians 4:8ff)

> Now abideth with you faith, hope and love—and the greatest of these is love. (I Cor. 13:1ff)

> But the fruit of the spirit is love, joy, peace, patience, kindness, goodness, faithfulness, gentleness, self-control; against such there is no law. (Galatians 5:22)

As I began researching for this chapter, I was reminded again and again how many times Paul the Apostle referred to the works of the spirit, of trying (testing) the spirit to see if it was of God or of man. The social activism so rampant in our time is too important to be left to the fanatics and the radicals. Very frequently, the activism is acting out some deep inner hostility, anger, and destructiveness. There was a time at the universities and colleges in America when the campuses were under siege. I remember talking to a campus minister and asking how he could justify his destructive anger. His response was that if the university or other institutions of America were burned down or destroyed, something better would arise in their place. How can we ever justify destructiveness to bring about peace or hope? Test all activism to see that it is motivated by love, justice, hope, and kindness, rather than an "acting out" of the inner demons and devils working within all of us.

The same applies to the current radicalism. There is no room in the Christian faith for bigotry, hatred, or persecution toward any person or groups of persons. Many, however, are attempting to use the church for their own purposes and promotion. Let us test such movements in line with our doctrines of responsible behavior, guidance of the Holy Spirit, and growth toward a more fully functioning human being who stands under the judgment of God and of life.

THE PASTOR AS COUNSELOR

All pastors are counselors. As Seward Hiltner used to say, "We do not have the option of whether or not to counsel; only the option of whether we will counsel wisely or poorly."

There is a significant difference between pastoral counseling and pastoral psychotherapy. Pastoral counseling is time-limited, goal-oriented, and restricted in scope. In many areas of America, seminaries are teaching prospective pastors to circumscribe their counseling. Four to six sessions seem to be the ideal length of time currently recommended by many Protestant seminaries.

One basic reason for this is the time limitation placed upon the pastor of a flock of 500 or 1,000 parishioners. To spend unlimited sessions with any parishioner is to take away from the time available for the general congregation.

Another basic reason is the reality of the limitations of training in psychological skills and techniques. Most pastors are not equipped to venture into the sanctity of the subconscious or to be alert to the nuances of transference and countertransference.

Another basic reason for time limitation is the reality of a litigious society in which pastors, well intentioned or not, are vulnerable to claims of impropriety or incompetency, regardless of how ethical and conscientious they may be.

There are many parishes that are isolated from metropolitan centers where specialized professionals are found. Pastors then may have placed upon them expectations to perform tasks for which they are unequipped. In that situation, the pastor becomes the coordinator of treatment, the triage professional, who must see that the best available treatment is provided.

Under these circumstances, well-trained parish pastors who are isolated from other resources take on the role of pastoral therapist. This may be done only with supervision and collaboration.

At this point, pastors must protect themselves and their churches from unjustifiable and unsubstantiated charges of abuse or even worse, quackery. Many ministers get into trouble by being naive about their own vulnerabilities and the litigious world in which we live.

Safeguards such as scheduled and documented appointments, having other personnel available, doors left ajar, structured meetings, and up-front discussion of role limitations should always be included. Well-intentioned pastors get into trouble as often as those who are less conscientious. Define your role and learn to adhere to limitations and guidelines as well as to exercise the strengths and prerogatives that you have.

One of the first lawsuits involving a church and a pastor centered around a man who committed suicide while having been in a counseling relationship with one of the pastors of his church. The man's family stated that the pastor did not have adequate training, did not take proper precautions to protect the parishioner, and did not warn the family of the danger involved. Needless to say, such a death is tragic. The pastor must at all times seek to protect the parishioner in a counseling relationship, as well as his church and his own professional integrity.

The shepherd of the flock, the pastor, stands in a unique and responsible role. People in pain may share with a pastor information, pain, and sorrow that would never be shared with another person. This special privileged and holy relationship should never be abused or taken for granted. Indeed, a pastor should enter into it reverently, discreetly, and in the awe of God.

There is nowhere in the New Testament an answer to the problem of evil. There are hints about how evil, sickness, and pain in our lives should be handled, but there is no theological or philosophical solution to the riddle of suffering. Therefore, the pastor should approach this area of life with humility and honesty, for it is one of the great mysteries of life. Life is an adventure to be lived rather than a puzzle to be solved. As Weatherhead indicated in his book of sermons by the same title, the key is next door.

Tomás Romero, a columnist for *The Denver Post*, writes of homeless youth and the Colorado General Assembly (state legislature): "Perhaps a few of those midnight massacre legislators should listen to the voice of a youth who said, 'People only see the spiked hair and chains; they don't see 'me.' If they could, they'd realize that the only difference between us is that I wear my pain on the outside.' "[2]

If I see any danger in the current pastoral care movement, it is in the area of setting aside a specialty that is neither truly pastoral nor truly psychological. From my vantage point, all pastoral counselors are pastors first, with experience in the parish and hospital, who have struggled and are struggling with their faith, and who bring the additional skills of psychology to their task and calling.

This group of pastoral specialists is not separated from the church, but rather should be an integral part of it. It is my hope and prayer that more parish pastors become part of the pastoral care and counseling movement rather than leaving it to specialists with very little training or experience in the pastorate. This is in no way intended to cast negative aspersions on professional pastoral counselors, but rather to seek to upgrade this specialty by grounding it in the parish church.

A few years back, there was discussion, even argumentation, about the nomenclature for theological school graduate degrees. Should the theological degree be called a Master of Divinity, a Master of Theology, a Doctor of Ministry, or a Master of Sacred Theology? The typical graduate theological program calls for three or four years of seminary beyond the bachelor's degree. Therefore, a Bachelor of Divinity was seen as inadequate recognition for such an extensive program.

Some recipients of the Master of Divinity degree went into counseling specialties and hung out their shingles-MDiv. A few would slowly decrease the "iv" part and all that was readable was the MD. This misleading grew out of feelings of insecurity and inferiority, attempting to identify with the medical model. Such practice became heavily frowned upon by church bodies who respected the significance of the calling of the pastor and did not seek to copy another profession's nomenclature or claim expertise that they did not have.

Pastors should hopefully gain some feeling of the significance of their calling and realize that it is one of integrity and competence that does not need to mimic or copy other profession's. Let pastoral counselors be a part of the church; let them develop true pastoral hearts that seek to be responsible shepherds of the flock. Let the pastoral counselors be grounded not only in psychological expertise, but also well grounded in their faith. To that end, they should intentionally and periodically reexamine what they believe as well as their own spirits for littleness or meanness. Let them possess their own souls in peace in order that they may truly guide others in this exciting journey of life.

A young college student with multiple sclerosis was being wheeled past one of the religious foundations when a woman came out of the center. She looked at the young girl in the wheel chair and said, "What terrible sin have you committed that God would punish you in this way?"

This chapter has focused on one theme: perhaps a plea to deeply examine your theology, not those ideas which come from the textbooks or professors, but those beliefs which lie deeply embedded within your personal faith. Take a long look at what you believe and use that examination as a stimulus for growth.

If your theology centers around illness as a punishment from God for past sins, parental errors, or evil thoughts, then in the name of all that is holy and sacred, including human personality, reexamine your theological assumptions before you begin counseling with someone suffering from depression.

When we say that we know God through the incarnation of divine qualities and virtues, we are not saying that we can only know God in that way. I am convinced that "the still small voice" can come to us in moments of silence, meditation, seclusion, and prayer. We should, however, be aware that even these solitary methods are influenced by relationships of the past embedded deep into our subconscious. Even as we read the Scriptures, we must confess that the words are mediated by other persons who wrote the scriptural legacy that enhances our current journey.

Peter Bertocci, a philosopher and psychologist, wrote very powerfully of the concept of religion as creative insecurity.

Men, at their best, will worship a creative, redemptive God, and only this one. Any other they fear. Any other may seem to give security, but not the blessedness which forgiving love knows as a creative insecurity.

There are, of course, many other sides to religion and to Christian faith. If what emerges here is a conception of religion as creative insecurity versus "peace of mind," as blessedness versus "happiness," as moral maturity versus psychological "integration," as growth versus "rest," as forgiveness versus prudential goodness, it is because I believe that only a religion that accepts insecurity can destroy evil and purify life. There is a more profound religious psychology than most current psychological treatments of religion seem to realize.[3]

Chapter 9

The Minister's Own Mental Health

A favorite statement made by one of my seminary professors years ago was, "You are not here to get your little tin cups filled." It was not meant as harshly as it sounded. The intent was to point out that seminarians and clergy needed to take care of their personal and spiritual needs elsewhere. It was a reminder that we were in seminary to learn, not to be soothed or coddled. Our spiritual and emotional health were our own responsibility. It was up to us to see that our physical, emotional, and spiritual needs were met as wholesomely and realistically as possible.

Many pastors and priests have difficulty and weaken their therapeutic skills for the following reasons:

a. They are not in touch with themselves and are therefore not aware of their hungers, and at times, emptiness.

b. For varied reasons, they do not take time to expend the energy or funds necessary to fill their own cups.

c. They have no access to collegial support, interpersonal warmth, or internal strengths and resources.

d. They are closed to the acceptance of gifts and graces that are all around them.

Ministers cannot adequately be servants until they have first been served. We cannot teach what we do not know, any more than we can come back from a place we have not been. This statement is valid theologically as well as psychologically. The healthier we are spiritually and emotionally, the better we can minister to those seeking growth and wholeness (holiness).

There is a condition that Dr. Karl Menninger used to call "weller than well." Mental and spiritual health are not to be thought of as simply the absence of illness or pathology, but the possession and awareness of strengths and resources that energize the human being and allow creativity and the fullness that enables us to give of ourselves freely and wisely.

Certainly, at times, we minister in the presence of our own pain and emptiness. "Wounded healers" is not a new concept. We sometimes serve even when we are in personal struggle. Our ability to empathize and identify with struggling parishioners can be enhanced by our own search and struggle. Yet, unless we have our own journey on the right path and our own house in order, we can do more harm than good.

Several years ago, a playwright wrote about the legend of the pool of Bethesda. In this story, he tells about a physician who waits impatiently for the angel to make its appearance and to trouble the waters. The physician wants to be first in line so he can enter the disturbed waters and thus be healed of his own physical illness. But as he waits, a father comes to him and asks him to come to the house where his daughter sits in despondency. The father says, "Come, for only you can understand what she suffers, and only you can heal her." As he turns to leave, another man comes to the physician and says, "Physician, come and heal our boy, for only you who knows what suffering means can understand his infirmity." So as the physician turns, the angel comes and the physician hears a voice speaking as if only to him: "Draw back physician, healing is not for thee, for it is only you, who understands what pain and loneliness mean, who can reach out and heal the pain and loneliness of others."

Perhaps the message here is just this: When the hand of grief and death touches our lives, it brings with it a compassion for the suffering of others that nothing else can supply. It furnishes for us an awareness of the deep significance of life itself.

Counselors can be extremely harmful when they seek first to satisfy their own egotistical needs through the parishioner or counselee. Pastoral counseling serves best when members of the clergy can become free enough to put their own needs aside and focus on the human beings who have come to them for new strength. A person preoccupied with himself has extreme difficulty understanding or empathizing with another.

At one annual meeting of the American Association of Pastoral Counselors, a colleague used the phrase "the sacrament of human encounter." This is an overwhelmingly powerful concept once we understand its implications. The sacrament is that holy ceremony through which God can and does act. This encounter is greater than just two or more people responding, but is a sacred interaction that releases and empowers the Holy Spirit to move, heal, and bless. There is a quality that becomes present, or whose presence we become aware of, in this human interaction. "You shall love your neighbor as yourself" (Lev. 19:18).

> And he said to him, "You shall love the Lord your God with all your heart, and with all your soul, and with all your mind. And the second is like unto it, you shall love your neighbor as yourself." (Mark 12:31)

FALSE GOALS

Americans tend to worship many false deities with their commitment of time, loyalty, and financial resources. Some of these are the spurious idols of success, fame, achievement, recognition, wealth, acceptance, popularity, and the elusive one of happiness.

For a number of years, I was director of a state-funded mental health center. Often, people in distress would come into the mental health center asking for help. They would frequently weep and say, "I just want to be happy." This cry was so vague and general as to be meaningless. When asked to be a little more specific about their pain or emotional needs, they had difficulty in focusing on what they wanted or needed in order to make them happy.

The Bible speaks often of blessedness (*makarios*), but not happiness. Jesus did not imply happiness in the generally accepted sense when He gave the beatitudes. We must not confuse the giddiness of being happy with the inward stability of blessedness. The professor who talked about little tin cups also concluded the chapel service with, "And now may the peace of God, which the world can neither give nor take away, fill your hearts. . . ."

If you are happy in the presence and awareness of starvation in Somalia, something is wrong. Run, don't walk, to the nearest synagogue, temple, or church, and ask that God stab your soul awake with the pain and need in and of the world.

Yet, if you become immobilized and paralyzed or personally debilitated as you face the pain in the world, you cannot become part of the healing process.

> I listen to the agony of God
> I who am fed,
> I see the dead.
> The children starved for lack of bread.
> I see, and try to pray.
> I listen to the agony of God—
> I who am warm,
> Who never yet have lacked a sheltering home,
> In dull alarm
> The dispossessed of hut and farm,
> Aimless and transient roam.
> I listen to the agony of God—
> I who am strong
> With health, and love, and laughter in my soul,
> I see a throng
> Of stunted children reared in wrong,
> And wish to make them whole.
> I listen to the agony of God—
> But know full well
> That not until I share their bitter cry—
> Earth's pain and hell—
> Can God within my spirit dwell
> To bring his kingdom nigh.[1]

Blessedness and peace with power are as different from happiness as wisdom is from drunkenness. Even physical health is a goal that is not always attainable. We minister in and through our own illnesses, so long as we are aware of them and put them aside, in service of a greater cause—the healing and well-being of all mankind.

Paul Hauck has long been one of my favorite writers. His theories rely heavily on rational-emotive therapy as developed by Albert Ellis. Hauck is sensitive to the needs of pastors and laity within the church. He offers concrete, common sense guidelines toward changing our lives by changing our thoughts, attitudes, and behaviors. In 1988, he published a summary of his thinking as a clinical psychologist for the past several decades. One chapter deals with the problem of self-neglect. He states:

> People who suffer from self-neglect feel guilty about taking the slightest interest in themselves. As a consequence of this, they get depressed. They don't enjoy good health. They fail to use their money wisely. They let others trample all over them. They have few, if any, friends. They do not get the best out of life. Life in fact, passes them by.[2]

Hauck counters the problem of self-neglect by suggesting that we learn the art of enlightened self-interest. People, especially pastors, physicians, and psychologists who do not take adequate care of themselves, i.e., do not practice enlightened self-interest, cannot, over an extended period of time, take adequate care of their marriages, their families, or their churches.

Hauck approaches life as a do-it-yourself project. Mental health is within the reach of all of us who are willing to risk and learn some new behavior. Thoughts, ideas, and attitudes are as much behaviors as is physical exercise.

MINISTERS AND INAPPROPRIATE
SEXUAL INVOLVEMENT

Recently, a woman who identified herself as an author and psychotherapist informally linked to the church was found liable in a court of law for long-term sexual exploitation of one of her clients. The indications were that improprieties had occurred with many previous counselees. Televangelists, priests, and ministers are being held publicly accountable for their sexual transgressions as never before, as well they should be.

Many of them become naively involved because they are empty, hungry, and lonely. My personal experience and judgment would estimate that only a moderate percentage of clergy become too involved because of immorality or sociopathy. The more balanced and complete lives we can live, the more we will be able to eliminate the clergy's sexual abuse of their parishioners or counselees. Clergy members who are aware of their own problems and are in the process of solving them are less likely to strive to fulfill their personal needs in the intimacy and sanctity of professional relationships. Perhaps only priests, rabbis, pastors, or physicians enter as deeply into the inner depths of others' souls. It should never be done without realizing the holy ground upon which we as the clergy stand and with a humble awareness of our own weaknesses and vulnerabilities. We should never seek to meet our personal ego-needs through our parishioners or counselees.

A pastoral counselor from Georgia lists seven categories of vulnerable pastors. The first six are reported by psychologists Gonsiorek and Schoener in the *American Psychological Monitor.* The seventh category was added by Stephen Muse in the *Journal of Pastoral Care.* These basic categories are

1. the uninformed, naive pastor,
2. the pastor in personal crisis,
3. the severely neurotic minister,
4. the minister with psychosexual disorders,
5. the narcissistic or sociopathic minister,
6. the minister with undiagnosed chemical imbalance, and
7. the codependent pastor.[3]

The uninformed, naive pastor lacks adequate training, experience, or ongoing supervision in the standards of pastoral care and counseling, as well as adequate understanding of his own unconscious motivations and processes. The pastor is basically unaware of what he is doing to himself or to others. This pastor is more in need of guidance and direction than reprimand.

It becomes imperative that the denominational entity, the governing body, see that its ministers are adequately trained. Such competency is not optional, and should be considered a responsibility and a gift to both the minister being guided and the parishioner that is being offered competent, trained clergy. In the current professional scene, churches must take their responsibility to provide rigorous training for their professional representatives seriously. Seward Hiltner pointed out that clergy do not have the option to choose whether or not they counsel, only the option to counsel wisely or poorly.

Psychologists, psychiatrists, and other mental health providers can no longer slide by with either poor skills or evil intent. Not knowing or caring about what we are doing is as immoral as doing something that is intentionally hurtful. To be very blunt and direct about this issue, self-contented inefficiency or incompetency is immoral. We are given a resounding imperative to enhance our skills on every level. If the pastor or priest does not know what he or she is doing in the field of psychotherapy, they should seek those skills or refer parishioners to qualified professionals who possess the needed expertise.

Severely neurotic ministers draw their identity almost entirely from their work or feel compelled to gain the approval of parishioners rather than conscientiously serving their spiritual needs. The ministry then becomes a popularity contest. Ministers feel good about themselves when applauded and poorly about themselves when criticized. Some clergy have no identity outside of their role in the church. They spend most of their lives seeking the approval of "their people," their superiors, or whomever they look to for that inner sense of identity that they never find. This neurotic trait is one the pastor should address in his or her own therapy or with a trusted friend and insightful mentor. Who we are is separate from the popularity granted or denied to us by the crowd. It feels good to be liked. It feels painful to be disliked. But our worth and identity are more than transient praise or disdain.

A primarily healthy pastor, in a personal crisis such as an unhappy marriage or divorce, may trade on his woundedness to receive comfort from a parishioner. Because the pastor's ego strength is depleted due to unusual and painful circumstances, he seeks to get needs met in unacceptable and harmful ways. This pastor must discover access to his own resources rather than fill his loneliness or assuage his pain through people that turn to him in times of their personal needs. The ministry is a profession, perhaps one of the highest and holiest of professions, and clergy must assume responsibility for their actions as such.

The minister with a personality or psychosexual disorder lacks impulse control and tends to abuse many different victims in a repeating pattern. Unfortunately, this type will not read this book nor seek assistance for this problem. It then becomes incumbent upon the church body to protect the well-being of the parishioners and to seek whatever remedial action is necessary. All too often, authorities will ignore or deny this kind of problem until severe damage is done to many people, including the victim, the victim's family, the church, the clergy member, and the family of the clergy member. Administrative incompetency or uncaring indifference is as immoral as overt acts committed by a sick clergy member.

The narcissistic or sociopathic minister carefully plots the vulnerabilities of certain parishioners or other victims and exploits them deliberately. It is well known that heterosexual or homosexual sex offenders and abusers seek out leadership or involvement with youth and children when this is the main area of their addiction. Hopefully, the percentage of such pastors is small. In faith bodies where there are few, if any, standards of conduct, the sociopathic pastor has a field ripe for the harvest, and takes advantage of those opportunities until some societal rule is violated. The church then becomes a symbol of ridicule and embarrassment. Narcissistic and sociopathic disorders are usually ego-syntonic; in other words, they do not produce psychological pain and the individual sees no reason to change or grow. Discipline and control must come from the outside.

Among the clergy members who become inappropriately involved are those with an undiagnosed chemical imbalance or mental disorder. They are out of control due to an organic brain syndrome or a mood disorder such as bipolar (manic-depressive) syndrome. Again, it becomes the responsibility of the ecclesiastical authorities to seek remediation. Clergy members who are ill are to be treated with the utmost compassion and care, just as we would hope the parishioners would and should be treated.

Some ill clergy have been treated as if they were moral lepers and rejected painfully in very uncompassionate and uncaring ways. The church, and we who claim to be involved in the healing of emotional pain, bear a responsibility to treat each other with respect, good will, and informed concern.

Clergy with Alzheimer's disease have often been shunted aside as if they had failed as human beings. Mental illness or organic brain disease should be treated in the same manner that we would treat any other malfunction of the human organism, with professional skill and intelligent caring.

Muse also adds a seventh category of the codependent or addictive personality. Without realizing it, this pastor is essentially and unconsciously attempting to control self "and others in various ways to meet his unacknowledged dependency needs."[4] This dependent and codependent pastor has an overwhelming need to be needed. Through his or her attempts at control, the pastor reduces his or her personal anxiety and the risk of being unnecessary.

HUMANISTIC PSYCHOLOGY

Humanistic psychology has greatly enhanced our understanding of the healthy personality. Carl Rogers points out that the "good life" is a process, not a destination. "The good life is the process of movement in a direction which the human organism selects when it is inwardly free to move in any direction."[5]

Four strands that weave together into the fabric of increasing health are:

1. openness to experience,
2. being alive in the present moment,
3. not becoming overwhelmed with guilt from the past or anxiety over the future, and
4. increasing trust in ourselves rather than reliance upon judgment of others.

If 15 percent of the population, or about 32 million individuals, have a mental illness, what about the other 85 percent? Are they to be considered "mentally healthy"? From the point of view that defines normality or mental health as the "absence of a diagnosable disorder," those 85 percent are to be regarded as "normal" or "mentally healthy." However, very few mental health professionals or social scientists would accept this conclusion. Rather, it is widely accepted that health is not just the absence of disorder. The mental health field, and increasingly the general health field, are not satisfied with the goals of reduced mortality, morbidity, or even the elimination of illness; they have attempted to define more positive goals toward the *enhancement* of health.[6]

AN APPROACH TO PASTORAL WELLNESS

There are certain qualities in life to which pastors are entitled. At the same time, these qualities enhance pastoral leadership because they help pastors find strength and wisdom to give meaningfully and profoundly to those who turn to them for spiritual guidance.

Exuberance

Now and then, there needs to be room enough in life for the singing of angels. There is sheer joy in being alive, a gladness as we breathe in the clean air of a magnificent day. This joy puts one in touch with life all around—life overflowing with beauty even in the midst of ugliness. Exuberance is experienced only in brief episodes or glimpses. These moments are so rare and wonderful we need to store them in our memory bank where they can be accessed in times of routine, drudgery, and ordinariness.

We could not live on the hypomanic heights of ecstasy or exuberance anymore than we could live on a diet of hot fudge sundaes. Martin Luther King Jr. knew what it was like to have been to the mountaintop, to experience a great vision, but he also knew he would have to come down from such holy experiences to live, walk, and breathe in the streets and alleys where other human beings live. But if life does not have its redeeming moments of sheer delight, or we do not have time for the singing of angels or mystical experiences, our lives become tedious, dreary, and devoid of meaning. We must make time and room in our lives for the experience of exuberance, the peace with power that is beyond human understanding.

Stability

I was once summoned to testify in court as an expert witness on behalf of a state department of mental health. A family was seeking a commitment for an adult sibling who was obviously suffering from severe mental problems. In that hearing, I mentioned that the person in question was relatively stable. The angry family responded that this could not be the case due to the sibling's obviously strange behavior. When Freud used the term "stable," he did not mean that the personality was well or whole. He meant rather that the personality was not labile, in a state of flux or change. Stability, in and of itself, is never by itself a measure of mental health.

A person may be organized at a self-centered level of adaptation, with base motives and values, and still not be healthy. Stability, in the sense that I am using it here, means more than fixation at one level. Stability in the spiritual and emotional sense means the ability to stay the course, stick with the job, finish the task, and endure insignificance and pettiness in order to accomplish a goal. It is constancy with vitality. Stability implies the power to endure the experience of adversity without giving up or caving in. It is the power of inner strength to stand when the north wind blows.

Some pastors solve their problems by running to another parish, another assignment, a different relationship, or marriage. The difficulty in running away is that you always take yourself with you. If there are problems to be solved in a current situation, they need to be resolved where you are, if at all humanly possible.

Stability in the richest sense means an achieved balance in the warring factions of the personality so that one can be steadfast in the face of adversity.

Potentiation

This is the ability to develop the power and strength within us. Many of us are bound by old habits and life patterns that keep us from realizing the potential within us. Psychotherapy is all about finding power, sources of energy, and becoming strong enough to utilize more of that energy from within which is unique to each individual. Unless pastors are able to tap into their own source of being, to find their own voice, to sing their own song, regardless of the key, they remain robots dancing to another's tune. Each individual is born with many strengths if he can but get in touch with them. Becoming mentally well is a process of finding our strength, our own voice, and utilizing it to the fullest in light of the attenuating and extenuating factors of reality.

Freedom

Freedom to be who and what we are must be an essential ingredient of all mental health. Wearing masks, erecting defenses, and playing "as if" all detract from the ability to grow, expand insights, and express our true selves. I use the plural of self intentionally at this point because all of us are many selves, many different personalities. To become free to choose which self we place in control is a major function of maturity.

We need freedom from preoccupation with self. Harry Emerson Fosdick, in his writings refers to this as "getting one's self off one's hands." When we are saturated with self-concern, we do not have the capacity to truly understand another person nor empathize with what he or she is experiencing at the moment. Good pastors have that unique power to experience within themselves some of the pain and anguish that is within other people. They may essentially, for at least a short period of time, "walk within their moccasins" and reach out to them with true compassion.

William Henry Bernhardt was one of my major philosophical heroes. He had no use for paradoxes or dilemmas. Dr. Bernhardt used to say that a paradox was simply a problem that people did not think through, a result of mental laziness. To a point, this perspective has held true in my own experience, but I find room for many paradoxes in existence. There is a paradox surrounding freedom and empathy. If we identify so strongly with our parishioners, we become immobilized and can no longer function as separate, professional individuals. If, on the other hand, we cannot glimpse into the world of another person, our objectivity has robbed us of our most powerful tool—our common humanity.

Helping persons must solve some, if not most, of their own problems before they can adequately become informed helpers. Freedom from the past and its tyranny becomes a foundation for freedom to live fully in the present moment. To let go of the pain, or even success of the past, allows us to enter the "eternal now" with courage, faith, and hope. Letting go of the past that gets in our way may require professional help as well as soul searching, but it becomes a task that is our personal responsibility.

Freedom must also entail freedom from the future, perhaps more adequately expressed as freedom from the fear or anticipation of the future. We can become so future-oriented that "this eternal now" is missed because we are elsewhere. Fear of the future may be expressed in severe anxiety. Anticipation of the future may be experienced as putting off today because, at some time yet to come, we will be free to live, love, or help. Letting go of the past and the future, and living in the opportunities and realities of this day, becomes a matter of discipline and direction. "Nothing should be prized more fully than the living of this day" (Goethe).

> Wouldn't it be wonderful to recapture the imagination and wonder of the natural child? To feel once again the spontaneity, creativity, and excitement of life? To be able to explore and look and hear and taste and touch and smell? To be open to the world around you? To be able to waste a little time, turn off the clock, overcome hang-ups, to accept yourself as a worthwhile person? To appreciate the association with others? To drink from the satisfying waters of happiness, joy, and satisfaction?[7]

Insight

Insight is the core ingredient in becoming a solid and effective pastor. One basic reason why so many pastors get into trouble and so few parishioners get helped is that the shepherd of the flock lacks insight into his or her own behavior, and does not seek it out. All human beings employ defense mechanisms to protect them from overwhelming anxiety. Pastors, of all people, need to examine their own motives and become aware of some of their unconscious processes. By the very nature of being unconscious, they do not readily come to the surface.

For example, our need to be omnipotent takes away some of our feeling of insecurity. Our altruism may indeed cover some deeper-rooted feelings of hostility: "See, I am not hostile, I am feeding the hungry." An adequate awareness of some of our inner drives can greatly enhance our ministry and move us in the direction of being intelligent helpers rather than well-meaning bumblers.

There is the example of the parishioner who comes to the pastor with a deep-seated depression in the absence of significant depressive factors in the environment. The man has a good job, money in the bank, a stable marriage, and healthy children. He is respected and involved in many worthwhile activities, yet he remains depressed and has continuing feelings of self-deprecation. After exploring the inner world of the parishioner, the pastor may try to pray away the blues, or chastise the person for being "down" when he has so much, or encourage the man to stop feeling sorry for himself and give thanks for all that he has. While the advice might be appropriate in some situations, it may seriously compound the parishioner's problem. He may already be trying as hard as humanly possible and now the pastor has made the situation worse by adding more burden with instructions that do not work. The pastor, in this case, rather than being an objective, skilled helper, has a sense of omnipotence and wants to be the healer, rather than see that the parishioner is healed.

The depressed individual has an endogenous (coming from within) depression that needs to be treated medically. Reassurance, chastisement, and easy advice are to no avail in this situation. The pastor is attempting to do something that cannot be done that way. His motive on the surface may be benign, but guided introspection and proper training will help the pastor realize that his need to be needed, to demonstrate power, and to be significant have outweighed what is truly best for the parishioner seeking help.

The second example is like the first. A female parishioner comes to the pastor, telling him how marvelous he is. She gets more out of the sermons than ever before and thinks the pastor is so helpful in the classes he teaches and the prayers that are said. The parishioner then begins to express some long-standing needs and feels that the pastor is the only one who has the answers to her problems. Because the pastor's ego needs stroking, he gets "hooked" into believing how marvelous and skilled he is, and how insightful the parishioner is to recognize his brilliance. The pastor has been seduced in a nonsexual way into taking the bait—hook, line, and sinker. Insight into the pastor's own ego needs can go a long way toward keeping the pastor from doing too much, or taking on roles that are not appropriate.

Every pastor needs a personal consultant who is trusted enough to share concerns with and from whom to seek insight. This consultant should be removed from the ecclesiastical hierarchy and therefore neutral from an administrative point of view. Such sharing should be collegial, rather than over-under in the relationship. Some counseling sessions could be taped for further review, for insight, and to see what progress, if any, was being made.

In one such case, very little growth in the parishioner had taken place, although the woman was kept from suicide for several years.

When one symptom was removed, another would arise to take its place. When one problem was solved, another would magically spring up. In sharing tapes of latter interviews, the puzzled colleague asked a very meaningful question: "Does this client have to be sick in order to get to come into the center for counseling?" This was the case, since in order to qualify for the services of the center, a mental health need had to be specified. Once this insight was gained, the counselor and the counselee could move on to seeing that the person's needs for support were met in a more helpful and wholesome way, and outside long-term support could be sought and found. Termination could then take place. In this case, without insight, the counselor would have continued in a nonhelpful way to fill egotistical needs that should not have been met in the therapeutic situation.

The Menninger Foundation has been a pioneer in mental health for nearly a century. This great institution has been devoted not only to healing the sick, training future and present health professionals, and providing continuing research and education, but also to the prevention of mental illness and the enhancement of mental health. The following is their Criteria of Emotional Maturity:

- The ability to deal constructively with reality.
- The capacity to adapt to change.
- A relative freedom from symptoms that are produced by tensions and anxieties.
- The capacity to find more satisfaction in giving than receiving.
- The capacity to relate to other people in a consistent manner with mutual satisfaction and helpfulness.
- The capacity to sublimate, to direct one's instinctive, hostile energy into creative and constructive outlets.
- The capacity to love.[8]

The Christian pastor must realize that he or she has no special privileges and, indeed, should want none. Emotional maturity and mental health are goals to be sought. They are not objectives easily obtained. It is in the seeking that we obtain fulfillment, not in the arrival at a fixed destination. Let us therefore strive toward meeting our obligations as pastors and as human beings, and find growth and meaning in the journey.

Chapter 10

Taking Charge of Your Life

In the final analysis, all religion has to do with possessing one's own soul. Religion is the search for empowerment, for meaning, for the message that one's life has significance beyond just the bodily weight of being human—beyond this time and this moment. All religion is a search for a guarantee or a guarantor of values: our values, our life, our meaning.

During my first semester in seminary years ago, we invited a local radio personality to speak to an assembly of professors, ministers, and graduate students. Although he went by a pseudonym of "Lingo the Drifter," he turned out to be an erudite, sensitive man seeking to go back to nature and an elemental form of living. He was educated, I believe, at the University of Chicago and had a master's degree in sociology. Being a musician and disk jockey, he acted somewhat overwhelmed, at least on the surface, by being in the presence of so many clergy and clergy-to-be types. He slowly and methodically strummed his guitar and said, more to himself than anyone else: "You know, theology ain't worth a damn unless it hits a man in his life space."

Professors and theologians could have learned a great deal if they had paid serious attention to this quiet man who had great insight into human nature. Theology does not ring with resonance, does not have power and motivating force, unless it relates to where we live and move and have our being. It ain't worth a damn if it don't hit us in our personal experience.

The first step toward taking charge of our lives is to recognize that there are large areas of decision and control that belong to us as individuals. When we feel or become powerless, we have little hope that we can control some of our actions, words, thoughts, and emotions. We must begin with the knowledge that we are never completely helpless or hopeless to make the next decision or take the next step.

Ministers may become paralyzed or useless in either one of two ways. The first is where the minister gets caught up in the sound of his own voice and becomes an actor upon the stage. His sermons are performances. His human contacts are not genuine, emotional "meeting of meanings," but rather acts in which others are to respond to him as the great thespian of all time who is bringing the booming "Word of God" through his brilliance and profundity. In the final analysis, this performance can be overwhelmingly frightening; therefore, the minister must utilize all the defense mechanisms at his commands to keep this awareness from breaking through to consciousness—either his or his parishioners'. The pastor becomes a poseur, wearing a mask of certainty where there is no certainty.

The second position is nearly the opposite of the first. A pastor becomes painfully aware that she represents God, at least to the parishioner. In this powerful role, she becomes paralyzed and has difficulty functioning. She realizes how inadequate she is for the task. Final answers are not hers, the knowledge of the solution to all social problems escapes her, and there are psychological truths beyond her grasp. In this awareness of her own inadequacy and frailty, the pastor dies the death of a thousand qualifications. She does not move to the right or the left because either could be wrong.

So too, most of us can become terrified in life, play acting "as if" on one hand, or paralyzed into inactivity on the other. It is with the awareness of our finiteness that we are finally able to grasp the reins of our own lives and take charge in the areas given to us to decide, to act, and to be fully alive and fully human. We have received the gift of accepting our limitations and becoming responsible for whatever realm falls within our scope of decision making.

The Institute for Personality and Ability Testing has developed a short inventory called the Health Attribution Test. The test (the use of the term inventory or instrument is preferable) helps the subject determine how he relates to his own health issues, such as cardiovascular fitness. One major category of health attribution is to place the responsibility on significant others. These significant and powerful others are given power by us and authority over how we live, how our health is or becomes, and we leave much of the decision making in their hands. Also, we can blame them if things do not get better. In this category, we find the largest segment of the American population developing the cult of medical chauvinism. The medical doctor with the aid of the registered nurse will tell us what pill to take, and we become resigned to follow their wisdom, as if they were more than human and had the latest revelation from Mt. Olympus (or Mt. Sinai) regarding our health and healing.

A second category of health attribution is in the area of chance, fate, or "que sera, sera"—whatever will be, will be. If we are obese, it is a matter of chance. If we get lung cancer, it is not from smoking—it is from the statistical probability in the universe that this illness simply occurs to so many people and we were at the wrong place at the wrong time. This position would strongly indicate that we have little control over the events influencing our personal health. Wellness is a matter of chance, and if we are fortunate and have good genes (or grandparents or parents), we will then be healthy.

One of the modern profanities or perhaps obscenities is the whine, "It's not my fault. I couldn't help myself." Some criminal behavior is undoubtedly due to mental illness, severe personality disorders, or disturbances from a society gone awry. But to use the phrase, "It's genetic" is a cop out to keep us from facing our responsibilities.

Obviously, the third position is one that espouses individuals to take control of their own health issues. We determine what we put in our mouths, how many hours of television we watch, how much alcohol we consume, how many cigarettes we smoke, how little exercise we get, and eventually, within limits, our basic attitudes and emotions.

An interesting side note to this revealing instrument is that many professionals, clergy, psychologists, physicians, and nurses do not make good patients simply because they overreact. They neither take medication when necessary, nor do they heed the advice of specialists who may provide guidance for them. There always needs to be a balance, an understanding about what falls within our purview and what areas lie within the realm of the expertise of other helping professionals.

When we leave health choices to powerful others, we surrender our lives to perhaps well-meaning people who may approach us mechanically and methodically without listening to the total person. We have a spirit, a mind, and a will, as well as a body. The entire person must be viewed as a whole. Remember the earlier story of the "gall bladder on the seventh floor." Individuals may lose their names and identities and become simply another patient in room 793.

When we abdicate responsibility for our lives, we begin to believe in chance factors as being all determinative. When examined closely, this position is a shirking of responsibilities in favor of blaming the universe, fate, chance, or whatever other term you want to use.

There certainly are accidental occurrences in life. Surely, cancer can strike out of the blue. However, we are beginning to learn more and more that we can influence our health, including our mental health, in more ways than we ever thought humanly possible. We can influence our depression by our lifestyle, by our mental attitude, and by our volitional choices. Taking charge of our lives begins by assuming control of our health decisions. This may mean selecting physicians or psychologists or other professionals who are not only understanding but who will help us regain control over our body and mind.

In an analogy from transactional analysis, when we activate a healthy and functional adult, the ego gets in the driver's seat. The ego may activate the nurturing or critical parent as needed; the ego may decide that the playful child needs more recreation; the ego may also decide that all three ego states are needed for healthy functioning and may learn to schedule time and energy for each. In the way that we budget our money, let us learn to budget our stress. Let us learn when to play, how to work, and how to live fully in an exciting and challenging world. Creative and responsible living is not for sissies. Remember that. The race is not always to the swift, but it is always to those out there trying, making decisions, and making mistakes. The only saints are the sinners who keep on trying.

TAKE CHARGE OF YOUR TIME

One thing that Robert Dole, Newt Gingrich, and William Jefferson Clinton have in common with you is that each possess 168 hours in his week. They have no more and no less time than you or I have. Their days are divided into twenty-four hour periods, and their hours into sixty minutes. That fact always reminds me that the use of my time is very significant. The budgeting of a person's minutes and hours is one of the keys to creativity and productivity.

Most of us waste vast quantities of time each day and each week. When we add up the hours that are not creatively used, we usually become appalled at what could have been done or accomplished had we made other choices.

Life is a matter of priorities and choices. At the end of our days, we will begin to look back and see where we wish we had spent more energy and time. *Time usage is our gift to the world.* As I look back on some forty years of ministry, I at times resent every hour spent in useless committee meetings instead of with my wife, children, or friends. A rabbi once said that no one ever says in his final years that he wished he had spent more time at the office. So many successful and productive women and men have spent hour after hour getting an education and striving for recognition, acceptance, or financial security that they forgot what is truly important in life.

Jesus regularly called the disciples back to their priorities. "What shall it profit a man (or woman) if he (or she) shall gain the whole world and lose his soul?" (Mark 8:36). The paraphrases from that one sentence can be powerful. What if a man becomes the senior pastor of his denominations' largest church and loses his self-respect? What if a man becomes the cheerleader for the entire community and is beloved by the multitudes, but cannot talk to his own son? What if one of us fulfills our ambitions for achieving success and does not have the genuine affection and respect of our own spouse? Our measurement and feeling of success is always determined by the priorities we set for ourselves.

Benjamin Franklin, at the age of twenty-four, pondered long and hard on what constituted a superior human being. He decided at that age, he would seek "moral perfection" and established that as his goal. Sounds like John Wesley, doesn't it? ("Are you going on to perfection in this life?") Franklin said in his autobiography that he wished to live without creating any fault at all—a noble, although impossible and self-centered goal. Among the virtues he listed were temperance, silence, order, resolution, frugality, industry, sincerity, justice, moderation, cleanliness, tranquility, chastity, and humility. Benjamin Franklin had enough insight and sense of humor to be aware of the danger of becoming proud of his humility.

He discovered that he had undertaken a task more difficult than he had imagined, and therefore set about methodically to correct his vices and strengthen his virtues one at a time. He devised a journal where he made seven columns, one for each day of the week, and one page for each one of his virtues. He therefore felt he could keep track of his behavior and that in thirteen weeks, he would have covered thirteen virtues. This would allow him to go through his self-improvement course four times during the year.

> My intention being to acquire the habitude of all these virtues, I judged it would be well not to distract my attention by attempting the whole at once, but to fix it on one of them at a time, and when I should be master of that, then to proceed to another, and so on till I should have gone through the thirteen. And as the previous acquisition of some might facilitate the acquisition of certain other, I arranged them with that view as they stand above.[1]

Taking charge of your life means taking charge of your time rather than time taking charge of you. There is no better way to start than by ordering your priorities in life. At this point, we want to become brutally honest with ourselves. It may even be helpful to enlist the aid of a partner, intimate and trusted friend, a spouse, or ecclesiastical colleague or counselor. Whether another person is chosen or not, we need to be as up front as possible about what is truly significant in our lives. For what are we willing to sacrifice? To what are we going to give this next hour of our life? When that hour has been expended, that portion of our life has been given away.

Howard Thurman has perhaps meant more to my personal devotional life than any other contemporary author. His writings help me keep life in some kind of perspective and find deeper sources of meaning that stabilize and invigorate. In seeking a more meaningful life, we must zealously preserve time for personal spiritual growth. Just because one technique works for some people does not mean it will work for others. Develop for yourself your own method of self-renewal, but budget that into your daily and weekly schedule.

For married Protestant clergy, the family should be in the top three items of priority. We all have seen too many clergy members who have time for their church, community, and societal roles, yet have not established personal and deep relationships within their own families. Our children are with us for such a brief period of time that laughing, playing, sharing, and talking with them must have urgent priority. If not, later in life, we will bemoan the distance from our children and wonder where and how that happened. I hasten to add that I hope pastors do not take a guilt trip about this, but simply become aware of how important our spouses and children are to us. Certainly, committees have to be run, groups have to be met, hands have to be shaken, but none of these even begin to approach the significance of our families.

Pastors are often aware of the time trap in which they are caught, but unaware of how to get out of it or what to do about it. Let me make some concrete suggestions as well as point out numerous good books available on time management.

First, establish a hierarchy of values. You can never know if you are on the right road or have arrived at your destination unless you know where you are going. How will you know you are "there" if you do not know where "there" is? We need to clearly seek out our priorities in life, and determine which things are the driving engines behind our actions. Often, when we examine our priorities, we find that they are not destinations we still choose to visit. We may go through a painful revision of our goals, motives, and allegiances.

Second, faithfully, even compulsively, keep a record of how you spend your days. In fifteen-minute segments, outline the activities which filled your day, from the time you awake to your bedtime.

Third, establish a target number of hours for each of the values in your hierarchy. For example, ask yourself how many hours each day or week you want to spend watching television. It is often frightening to look at the fact that we spend thirty to fifty hours a week in front of the television set for no apparent reason.

Fourth, compare how you spent your hours during the past week with your goal allocations.

Fifth, seriously and strenuously schedule the events of the upcoming week. Write in the major scheduled and unavoidable meetings and events that must be attended. Do not write in routine items at this point. If you have written down as your target goal for your family twelve quality hours and that coincides with your hierarchy of values, then schedule that many hours on your appointment calendar. Do the same with your scheduling of quality time with your spouse, if you are married. Follow this exercise rigorously, and do not change your appointments with spouse, family, or self except for unavoidable emergencies. Here, the clergy often deceive themselves and others and consider any routine decision at the church an emergency and therefore preempt their allotted time for things that really matter.

Do you remember the story in the Gospel of Matthew in which Jesus raised Jairus' daughter from the dead? Jesus had drawn aside with a few of his disciples for prayer and meditation. He evidently was fatigued from being with the multitude of people and went on a much-needed personal retreat with a few selected friends. Upon his return to shore, he was compelled toward the house of this leader of the synagogue, whose daughter was ill. En route, Jesus encountered a desperate woman who was tugging at the hem of his garment. She had spent her small amount of funds going from one doctor to another to no avail. Her faith led her to believe that if she could only touch the hem of Jesus' garment, she would be healed. In the press of the throng, she was able to touch the edge of his cloak.

> Jesus turned around and saw her, and said, "Courage, my daughter! Your faith has made you well." At that very moment, the woman became well. (Mt. 9:22 TEV)

The important thing to remember is that in the course of one emergency, he was interrupted with another. Such will always be the case when dealing with human needs.

But let's face it: We often declare minor events urgent when they could be done at another time. Schedule them or assign them to someone else.

TAKE CHARGE OF YOUR HEALTH

An unfit pastor or counselor has no business advising people to "get in shape" when he or she does not practice the principles of physical and mental wholeness. Beware the unfit counselor. That does not mean that we must all be examples of marathon runners in order to model health. We must, however, practice and embody the principles of a healthy life (body, spirit, and mind) before we expound the virtues of health and holiness to others.

An old friend used to say that there were only two kinds of pastors: those that worked themselves to death or the lazy type that slid by as easy as they could in life. This particular pastor died at an early age of a heart attack. As pastor of a large church, he felt he had to do it all himself. He was overly responsible and could not delegate; as a result, the world was deprived of the example of an excellent pastor, husband, father, and friend. Dispense with the myth of omniscience and begin with a thorough physical exam. Enlist the aid, not the dominance, of your personal physician in targeting the physical areas of your life that you want to improve. As the commercial says, "Not perfect, better."

Take that agenda seriously. Go over it with your spouse or closest friend. Enlist his or her assistance and cooperation. It is hard to diet with a hot apple pie waiting for you at the end of the day.

Schedule a follow-up appointment with your physician to review your agenda, your methodology of correction or improvement, and the progress you have made. Reduce medication to the level necessary. Include exercise, relaxation, recreation, and fellowship with friends in your daily and weekly schedule. By remaining or becoming well, you will be able to help more people for a longer period of time; and what is more, you will enjoy the trip.

TAKE CHARGE
OF YOUR PERSONAL RELATIONSHIPS

No person is so wealthy that he or she can afford to lose a friend. Real friends, true friends, are one of God's greatest gifts to us. Most of us acknowledge their importance, but like appointments with our families, busywork squeezes them out of our agenda. Right now, select ten people that you truly consider friends. Make decisions about whether you want to keep them or not. If the decision is that they are not worth the trouble, then cross them off your list. If, however, the decision is the opposite, then decide to cultivate your friendship as astutely as you would a garden, your own health, or your personal, devotional, and spiritual life.

Friends are the roses in our lives. Do not neglect them. If they do not respond or reciprocate, seek and cultivate new friends who are true and loyal. The songstress sings, "People that need people are the luckiest people in the world." I beg to differ. People who want people are the luckiest people in the world. Needing and wanting are two different emotional states. Friendship is never the exercise of dependent relationships, but an arena for the true sharing of what is beautiful, valuable, and worthwhile.

Recently, a medical professional received a long-distance phone call. His father had been driving the car with his mother in it. They were headed for an appointment. En route, the father had a stroke, lost control of his automobile, and collided with a tree. The father was killed on impact, but the mother lingered for over a week in the hospital before she died. When this man expressed the terrible pain of losing both parents within one week, he said that he had called ten friends and urged them, if they had not already done so, to call their parents and tell them how much they were loved. Most of us need to do that with family and friends on a more frequent basis.

THE SPIRITUAL LIFE

Of all the areas of our lives, the spiritual dimension for the pastor must take high priority. Interestingly enough, the spiritual life is never separated from other dimensions of our life such as the emotional, volitional, educational, interpersonal, and physiological dimensions. Although distinct and discrete, spiritual life is and must always be dynamically interrelated to all of life and the universe in which it exists. We live, move, and have our being in a contextual setting that can never be ignored.

> I sought my soul
> my soul I could not see.
> I sought my God,
> my God eluded me.
> I sought my brother (sister)
> And I found all three.
> My God, my brother (sister), and me.
>
> (author unknown)

Each of us has his own definition of spiritual well-being. It seems that we approach it from a different angle. The spiritual dimension of my life centers around a faith in God, and a personal experience of being close to or far from that God. It involves being very deeply at home in (or grounded in) the universe, both material and spiritual, of which I am a part. The spiritual dimension also is intricately related to how I am now, have been in the past, and want to be in the future, related to my fellow human beings. The spiritual dimension of my life must scrutinize whether I am on target as I seek to do the will of God for my life. I am truly blessed in so many ways. My responsibilities have to come to grips with whether or not I am contributing something back to this world and using whatever wisdom or ability I may have to enhance the welfare of the human race. Is the model of the Christ clear enough in my mind, and do I seek to capture that spirit and share it with the world?

Rather than being presumptuous about describing my spiritual dimension, my intent here is to get you to focus long and hard on this part of your life. As we schedule urgent church and business appointments, let us set aside some time each day to delve deeply into the spiritual arena of our inner being. Prayer, meditation, scripture, confession, acceptance are mandatory parts of our individual life.

GETTING RID OF ANXIETY

One method of controlling and delimiting anxiety, worry, sadness, and anger (and other negative emotions) is to learn how to schedule them into life. Once the emotions that we label as negative or unpleasant have been accepted, we can make conscious and informed decisions about how much time we want to spend with them. Many people struggle with their anger until it eats a hole in their stomach. They deny their rage or bitterness and stuff it into the subconscious, but it is still there. Once we can acknowledge that rage, anger, fear, anxiety, and other bothersome emotions are put there for a reason, we can learn to manage them.

One bitter young man came to a mental health family center obsessed with a wrong that had been done to him. He was embittered to the degree that it was sapping his energy and robbing him of the present and the future. When we went over his daily routine, he realized the extent to which his bitterness was hurting him. He was then told to decide on the length of time he wanted to spend each day ruminating about what had happened. He responded, as most do, by thinking the exercise was silly. Finally, we came up with the figure of one hour that was to be allowed for worry and rumination. He was told to schedule one hour each day, in his appointment book, to be set aside for just this purpose alone. He was also told this would be adjusted up or down after one week of trial.

After one week of trial, he found that one hour was not necessary in one block of time, and so divided his anxiety schedule into two daily twenty-minute sessions. He was taught to do the best job of worrying as possible and to write down everything he could do and change about the past. After two more weeks of this exercise, he was taught "thought-stopping" techniques. This allowed him to interrupt anxiety, anger, and bitterness during the daytime. He would tell himself that it had to be reserved for one of his regular sessions. If he needed to, he could write it down on a note sheet and bring it up at the scheduled evening session.

He learned that worrying as effectively as possible eliminated the need to carry a twenty-four hour burden of hostility. Slowly, he realized that some of these negative emotions were unproductive, and they began to drop by the wayside. He no longer denied or stuffed his anger, nor did he allow it to dominate the new opportunities of his life. Slowly, he spiritually moved from death to life, from hate to love, from sadness to newness of life. We need to schedule time in our lives for worry, anger, and sadness and to confine the expenditure of our emotions to only those private moments.

Taking charge of our lives is an exciting adventure. If we do not do it, someone or something else will. There are numerous institutions, causes, and pressures that can easily dominate us, if we let them. In the final analysis, we can learn to possess our own souls, and thereby be free to give ourselves away to causes worthy of the best in us. In other words, we will be free to do the will of God.

As in dealing with others, we must focus on potential, not pathology. The growing edge of our lives is where we are now. The priorities and choices we make will determine where we go from here, and what we are yet to become.

Always focus on potential, not on pathology. In yourself, and in others—for all are children of God.

Chapter 11

Summary

Recently, while I was teaching a second-level psychology course to students whose ages varied from nineteen to fifty, we came to the inevitable chapter on Freud. The students were struggling with concepts of id, superego, libido, and the Oedipal complex. Many teachers, psychiatrists, behaviorists, and countless others, including some pastors, have tried to abolish or reject Freud and his ideas. Regardless of our reactions to him, we must be aware of the pioneering genius of this man who explored the human mind in a way that it had never been studied before.

No one specialty has a monopoly on the province of humankind. Psychiatrists come at the problem of understanding personality from one perspective, teachers from another point of view, psychologists from a third. Pastors or theologians approach it from still another dimension. Each has a legitimate place within our body of knowledge. We all need each other. Insights gained by one group become part of the matrix out of which the next set of ideas shall be developed. Unfortunately, suspicions and hostilities have arisen between and among specialties, along with some intense territorial jealousies and imperatives.

Depression may be primarily a biochemical response to stress or an expression of genetic inheritance. Depression may also be a learned phenomenon. It may, and usually does, have psychological implications that need to be addressed. The "soul" or "spirit" of human beings is profoundly affected by mental and physical illness.

The clergy, in order to most ethically and professionally minister to their parishioners, must be knowledgeable about depression and other forms of mental illness. It is to be treated as any physical illness would be treated: with kindness and competency.

Depression is neither a sign of weakness, nor of moral decay, nor a punishment from God.

Pastors should seek and cultivate every opportunity for strong, professional collegial relationships of respect and mutual appreciation. Pastors need the psychiatrists and the psychologists on their treatment teams in order to serve their parishes and the people within them. Pastors cannot and should not go it alone. They must surrender their omnipotence and reach out to establish a professional network for their own sake as well as the sake of others.

Second, the pastor should recognize depression as varied (heterogeneous) in nature. The illness comes from many different sources, and may be precipitated by varying stressors. Just as each snowflake is unique to all the others, so people are all different and respond in a multitude of ways.

Perhaps the ultimate religious emotion is that of awe—awe at the universe, awe in the presence of life itself, and awe at the miracle, complexity, and beauty of human personality. Let us as clergy stand in awe of the courage, the loyalty, the self-sacrifice, and the love found in people, both normal and depressed, sick or healthy. Let us give thanks that we are a part, an awesome part, of this great adventure toward health and wholeness.

Depression is a prevalent illness that affects a large number of people. The cost in lives, happiness, productivity, family, and stress is enormous.

Depression is a very treatable illness. Medical and psychological sciences have taken giant strides in developing new medications, modern methodologies, and compassionate approaches in the treatment of this painful malady.

Pastors are unique and important health care providers and should accept their role with humility, power, and knowledge. They have a God-given imperative and responsibility to become competent in an area where millions of people are hurting spiritually, emotionally, mentally, and physically.

The team approach is mandatory to provide the most effective treatment and support for persons in need.

The human being is a dynamic, changing organism that cannot be divided into artificial segments of body-mind-soul-spirit. The whole being must be treated with respect, dignity, and awe.

The crowning glory of God is a human being who is fully alive. What a privilege it is to be a part of that quest and adventure.

Notes

Introduction

1. Arthur J. Snider, "Psychiatrists Fear Epidemic of Depression and Hopelessness" (Denver: *The Denver Post*, April 11,1972), 55.
2. Paul Popenoe, "Suicide Among Youth" (Los Angeles: *Family Life*, January-February, 1978, Volume 39, #7), 9.
3. *Merck Manual*, Sixteenth Edition (Rahway, NJ: Merck Research Lab, 1992).
4. Simeon Margolis, *The Johns Hopkins White Papers: Depression and Anxiety* (Baltimore: Johns Hopkins Medical Institutions, 1996).
5. U.S. Department of Health and Human Services. Rockville, MD: Public Health Service AHCPR PUB. 93-0551 (April 1993).
6. Depression Guideline Panel, U.S. Department of Heath and Human Services, 8: 387-394. *Depression in Primary Care*, Volume 2, Treatment of Major Depression (Rockville, MD: U.S. Department of Health and Human Services, 1993).

Chapter 1

1. Nora Varanese, Personal correspondence. (Also quoted in open letter in *The Denver Post*, November 12, 1995).
2. Philip B. Kunhard Jr., Philip B. Kunhard, III, and Peter W. Kunhard, *Lincoln* (New York: Alfred A. Knopf, 1992).

Chapter 3

1. Alice Miller, *The Drama Of the Gifted Child* (New York: Basic Books, 1981).
2. Ibid.
3. Silvano Arieta, *Handbook of Psychiatry* (New York: Jason Aronson, 1973), 348.
4. Martin Seligman, *Helplessness* (San Francisco: W.H. Freeman and Co., 1975), 9.
5. Jules Masserman, *Theory and Therapy in Dynamic Psychiatry* (New York: Jason Aronson, 1973).

6. Seligman, op. cit.
7. Erik Erikson, *Identity and the Life Cycle* (New York: W.W. Norton, 1963), 62.

Chapter 4

1. *Diagnostic and Statistical Manual of Mental Disorders IV* (Washington, DC: American Psychiatric Association, 1994).
2. Aaron Beck, *Cognitive Therapy of Depression* (New York: The Guilford Press, 1979).

Chapter 5

1. Albert Ellis, *Reason and Emotion in Psychotherapy* (Englewood Cliffs, NJ: Prentice-Hall, 1975). Reprinted with permission.
2. Paul Hauck, *Reason in Pastoral Counseling* (Philadelphia: Westminster Press, 1972), 47.
3. Albert Ellis and Robert Harper, *A New Guide to Rational Living* (North Hollywood: Wilshire Book Co., 1975), 23.
4. Romans 8:37, King James Version.
5. Aaron Beck, *Cognitive Therapy and the Emotional Disorders* (New York: International Universities Press 1962), 82.
6. The Beck Depression Inventory can be obtained by writing to: The Psychological Corp., 555 Academic Court, San Antonio, TX, 78204-2498.

Chapter 6

1. *New Webster's Expanded Dictionary* (Miami: P.S.I. Associates, 1992).
2. Peter Lewinsohn, Ricardo F. Munoz, Mary Ann Youngren, and Antoinette M. Zeiss, *Control Your Depression* (New York: Prentice-Hall, 1986).
3. Ibid, p. 22. Reprinted with permission.
4. Ibid, p. 26.
5. Ibid, p. 77.
6. William Faulkner (acceptance speech, 1950, p. 8). *Nobel Prize Library* (New York: Alexis Gregory, 1971).
7. Robert E. Alberti and Michael L. Emmons, *Your Perfect Right* (San Luis Obispo, CA: Impact Publishers, 1990).

Chapter 7

1. Roy W. Fairchild, *Finding Hope Again* (San Francisco: Harper & Row, 1980).
2. Seward Hiltner, *Ferment In Ministry* (Nashville: Abingdon Press, 1969), 4.

3. Binford W. Gilbert, "Campus Ministry," Unpublished Doctoral Dissertation (The University of Denver, 1973), 44.

4. Sam C. Webb, *Preliminary Technical Manual: An Inventory of Religious Activities and Interests* (Princeton: Educational Testing Services, 1968), 12.

5. Kenneth Underwood, *The Church, the University, and Social Policy* 2 volumes (Middletown, CT: Wesleyan University Press, 1969), 27.

6. Edgar Draper, *Psychiatry and Pastoral Care* (Englewood Cliffs, NJ: Prentice-Hall, 1965), 129.

7. Ibid.

Chapter 8

1. Kathryn Guthrie, "Models of God". (Decatur: *The Journal of Pastoral Care,* Volume 47, Spring 1993), 28.

2. Tomas Romero, *"When Good Causes Die Quickly"* (Denver: *The Denver Post* May 19, 1993), 7B.

3. Peter Bertocci, *Religion As Creative Insecurity* (New York: Association Press, 1958), xiii.

Chapter 9

1. Georgia Harkness, "The Agony of God". (Apparently, this poem is in the public domain, and was attributed to Georgia Harkness. Permission to use it was requested and received from Abingdon Press.)

2. Paul A. Hauck, *Reason in Pastoral Counseling* (Philadelphia: The Westminster Press, 1972).

3. Stephen J. Muse, "Faith, Hope and the Urge to Merge" (*Journal of Pastoral Care*, Volume 46, Number 3, Fall 1992).

4. Ibid.

5. Carl Rogers, *On Becoming a Person* (New York: Houghton-Mifflin, 1972).

6. Daniel Offer and Melvin Sabshin, Jr., *Normality and the Life Cycle* (New York: Basic Books, 1984) 330.

7. John K. Bontrager, *Free the Child in You* (Philadelphia: United Church Press, 1974).

8. William C. Menninger, MD, *The Criteria of Emotional Maturity* (Topeka: The Menninger Foundation, 1966). Reprinted with permission.

Chapter 10

1. Benjamin Franklin, *The Autobiography of Benjamin Franklin* (New Haven, CT: Yale University Press, 1964).

Index

Order Your Own Copy of
This Important Book for Your Personal Library!

THE PASTORAL CARE OF DEPRESSION
A Guidebook

_____ in hardbound at $29.95 (ISBN: 0-7890-0264-7)

_____ in softbound at $19.95 (ISBN: 0-7890-0265-5)

COST OF BOOKS_____	☐ **BILL ME LATER:** ($5 service charge will be added)
	(Bill-me option is good on US/Canada/Mexico orders only;
OUTSIDE USA/CANADA/	not good to jobbers, wholesalers, or subscription agencies.)
MEXICO: ADD 20%_____	
	☐ Check here if billing address is different from
POSTAGE & HANDLING_____	shipping address and attach purchase order and
(US: $3.00 for first book & $1.25	billing address information.
for each additional book)	
Outside US: $4.75 for first book	
& $1.75 for each additional book)	Signature_____
SUBTOTAL_____	☐ **PAYMENT ENCLOSED: $**_____
IN CANADA: ADD 7% GST_____	☐ **PLEASE CHARGE TO MY CREDIT CARD.**
STATE TAX_____	☐ Visa ☐ MasterCard ☐ AmEx ☐ Discover
(NY, OH & MN residents, please	☐ Diners Club
add appropriate local sales tax)	Account #_____
FINAL TOTAL_____	Exp. Date_____
(If paying in Canadian funds,	
convert using the current	Signature_____
exchange rate. UNESCO	
coupons welcome.)	

Prices in US dollars and subject to change without notice.

NAME _____

INSTITUTION _____

ADDRESS _____

CITY _____

STATE/ZIP _____

COUNTRY _____ COUNTY (NY residents only) _____

TEL _____ FAX _____

E-MAIL_____

May we use your e-mail address for confirmations and other types of information? ☐ Yes ☐ No

Order From Your Local Bookstore or Directly From
The Haworth Press, Inc.
10 Alice Street, Binghamton, New York 13904-1580 • USA
TELEPHONE: 1-800-HAWORTH (1-800-429-6784) / Outside US/Canada: (607) 722-5857
FAX: 1-800-895-0582 / Outside US/Canada: (607) 772-6362
E-mail: getinfo@haworth.com
PLEASE PHOTOCOPY THIS FORM FOR YOUR PERSONAL USE.

BOF96